MEDIA, FEMINISM, CULTURAL STUDIES

The Sacred Cinema of Andrei Tarkovsky
by Jeremy Mark Robinson

Liv Tyler
by Thomas A. Christie

The Cinema of Hayao Miyazaki
Jeremy Mark Robinson

Stepping Forward: Essays, Lectures and Interviews
by Wolfgang Iser

Wild Zones: Pornography, Art and Feminism
by Kelly Ives

'Cosmo Woman': The World of Women's Magazines
by Oliver Whitehorne

The Cinema of Richard Linklater
by Thomas A. Christie

Andrea Dworkin
by Jeremy Mark Robinson

Cixous, Irigaray, Kristeva: The Jouissance of French Feminism
by Kelly Ives

*The Erotic Object: Sexuality in Sculpture
From Prehistory to the Present Day*
by Susan Quinnell

Women in Pop Music
by Helen Challis

Sex in Art: Pornography and Pleasure in Painting and Sculpture
by Cassidy Hughes

Erotic Art
by Cassidy Hughes

Jean-Luc Godard: The Passion of Cinema / Le Passion de Cinéma
by Jeremy Mark Robinson

Genius and Loving It! Mel Brooks
by Thomas Christie

The Comic Art of Mel Brooks
by Maurice Yacowar

Marvelous Names
by P. Adams Sitney

The Art of Katsuhiro Otomo
by Jeremy Mark Robinson

Akira: The Movie and the Manga
by Jeremy Mark Robinson

The Art of Masamune Shirow (3 vols)
by Jeremy Mark Robinson

Detonation Britain: Nuclear War in the UK
by Jeremy Mark Robinson

Julia Kristeva: Art, Love, Melancholy, Philosophy, Semiotics
by Kelly Ives

Luce Irigaray: Lips, Kissing, and the Politics of Sexual Difference
by Kelly Ives

Helene Cixous I Love You: The Jouissance of Writing
by Kelly Ives

FORTHCOMING BOOKS

Legend of the Overfiend
Death Note
Naruto
Bleach
Hellsing
Vampire Knight
Mushishi
One Piece
Nausicaä of the Valley of the Wind
The Twilight Saga
Harry Potter

A CHINESE GHOST STORY
TONY CHING SIU-TUNG

A CRITICAL STUDY

A CHINESE GHOST STORY
TONY CHING SIU-TUNG

A CRITICAL STUDY

Jeremy Mark Robinson

CRESCENT MOON

Crescent Moon Publishing
P.O. Box 1312
Maidstone, Kent
ME14 5XU, Great Britain
www.crmoon.com

First published 2024.
© Jeremy Mark Robinson 2024.

Set in Helvetica 9 on 12pt.
Designed by Radiance Graphics.

The right of Jeremy Mark Robinson to be identified as the author of this book has been asserted generally in accordance with sections 77 and 78 of the Copyright, Designs and Patents Act 1988.

All rights reserved. No part of this book may be reprinted or reproduced, stored in a retrieval system, or transmitted, in any form or by any means, electronic, mechanical, photocopying, recording or otherwise, without permission from the publisher.

British Library Cataloguing in Publication data available for this title.

I.S.B.N.-13 9781861718785

CONTENTS

Acknowledgements ❖ 9
Picture Credits ❖ 9
Abbreviations ❖ 9

**PART ONE
BIOGRAPHY
TONY CHING SIU-TUNG
TSUI HARK**

1   Tony Ching Siu-tung: Biography ✱ 14
2   Aspects of the Cinema of Tony Ching Siu-tung ✱ 32
3   Tsui Hark ✱ 61

**PART TWO
A CHINESE GHOST STORY**

1   *A Chinese Ghost Story* ❖ 81
2   *A Chinese Ghost Story 2* ❖ 107
3   *A Chinese Ghost Story 3* ❖ 116
4   *A Chinese Ghost Story: The Tsui Hark Animation* ❖ 125
5   Movies Related To *A Chinese Ghost Story* ❖ 142

Filmography ❖ 150
Recommended Books and Websites ❖ 164
Bibliography ❖ 165

ACKNOWLEDGEMENTS

To the authors and publishers quoted.
To the copyright holders of the illustrations.

ABBREVIATIONS

LM *The Cinema of Tsui Hark* by Lisa Morton

PICTURE CREDITS

Golden Harvest. Shaw Brothers. Paragon. Cinema City. Film Workshop. China Entertainment. Paka Hill. Eastern Production. Win's Entertainment. Star East. Jing Productions. Media Asia. Beijing Polyabana Publishing. United Filmmakers Organization. China Film Co-Production. Big Pictures. China Juli Entertainment Media. Distribution Workshop. Different Digital Design. Huxia Film Distribution. New Classics Pictures.

NOTE

Parts of this book appeared in my full-length study of Tsui Hark: *Tsui Hark: Dragon Master of Chinese Cinema* (2023), published by Crescent Moon.

왕조현

인간과 귀신의
이룰 수 없는 사랑!

천녀유혼

장국영 주연

| 수입/제공 | 조이앤클래식

3월, 전설의 사랑이 다시 온다!

PART ONE
TONY CHING SIU-TUNG
TSUI HARK

1
TONY CHING SIU-TUNG: BIOGRAPHY

TONY CHING SIU-TUNG: INTRO

Tony Ching Siu-tung (b. 1953) started out as an actor and stuntman, working in movies in the late 1960s and 1970s; he moved into television as martial arts co-ordinator in the late 1970s and thru the 1980s (on several historical TV series); he moved up to directing movies with 1983's *Duel To the Death*.

Tony Ching Siu-tung's two signature works are probably *A Chinese Ghost Story* and *The Swordsman 2*. Critically, those two films (and their movie series, the *Chinese Ghost Story* series and the *Swordsman* series), have garnered the highest criticial accolades (and they were big hits financially), and *The Swordsman 2* has been the subject of numerous analyses of gender-bending issues in cinema. The sight of Brigitte Lin in drag and later fooling around with Jet Li as a 'woman' who was a man seems to drive film critics goo-goo.

Tony Ching Siu-tung has won top awards for the action choreography for *The Witch From Nepal, Shaolin Soccer, New Dragon Gate Inn, Hero* and *The Swordsman*.

Like the other famous action directors in Hong Kong cinema (such as Yuen Woo-ping, Sammo Hung, Corey Yuen Kwai and Yuen Bun), Tony Ching Siu-tung has worked with every single star in Hong Kong, every producer, every cameraman, designer, stylist, costumier, etc, and probably every stuntman and stuntwoman.

Tony Ching Siu-tung has action director credits on: *Dangerous Encounter – 1st Kind, Twinkle Twinkle Little Star, Peking Opera Blues, A Better Tomorrow 2, The Killer, New Dragon Gate Inn, Moon Warriors, City Hunter, Butterfly and Sword*, the *Krrish* films, *Kung Fu Dunk* and *The Warlords*. He is an action director in high demand – for many TV shows as well as movies. Ching has worked many times with producer/ director/ dynamo Tsui Hark.

Tony Ching Siu-tung seems barely known outside of Chinese film circles, and in the West[1] his name is over-shadowed by directors such as Tsui Hark, John Woo, Wong Kar-wai, etc. Yuen Woo-ping has become known for the *Matrix* movies and others, and of course Jackie Chan remains a huge presence (tho' as a movie star, and not for his incredible directing skills. Few realize that Chan has directed several genuine masterpieces, including the *Project A* series and the *Police Story* series).

But consider the achievements of Tony Ching Siu-tung – they are very impressive: two of the finest and most celebrated of Hong Kong franchises – the *Swordsman* movies and the *Chinese Ghost Story* movies. Judged solely on the basis of those two film trilogies, Ching is a *kung fu* master and lion dancer among filmmakers. The first two *Chinese Ghost Story* films are masterpieces, as are the first two *Swordsman* films (some would include the third installment, too – it's very popular with critics and fans). Near-masterpieces would include Ching's first film as director, *Duel To the Death, The Sorcerer and the White Snake, Jade Dynasty* and *An Empress and the Warriors*. Add to those giant historical pictures his work as action director on masterpieces such *Hero, Peking Opera Blues, House of Flying Daggers, A Better Tomorrow 2* and *The Killer*, and a host of very enjoyable pictures, such as: *Butterfly and Sword, City Hunter, Moon Warriors*, the *Krrish* films, *Curse of the Golden Flower,* and *The Warlords*. (Some of those productions were enormous – *Krrish, The Warlords, Hero, Curse of the Golden Flower*, etc).

Technically, the movies directed by Tony Ching Siu-tung are breathtaking – in every department of film production, Ching's movies excel. Costumes are lavish, the sets are super-detailed, and the cinematography is stellar. Sometimes you really are looking at something very close to a classical, Chinese painting, where the billowing robes that the actors wear fit in perfectly, and are spot-on equivalents for the spiritual mood of Chinese art. The floating, ruffling clothes are also practical, on-set versions of the human figures in Chinese art, as if they have been animated from paintings on silk and given three-dimensional form.

Like Tsui Hark, Tony Ching is fascinated by visual effects, and his cinema contains every trick imaginable. Ching's cinema celebrates the magic of filmmaking, the artifice, the dream.

Talking about the issue of co-direction: Hong Kong cinema has a long-established tradition of sharing duties in many areras of production, direction included.[2] The high speed of production meant that if someone wasn't available, someone else would step in; it was simply a practical solution; the idea of waiting weeks until the main director became available again, because only the main director was capable or legally authorized to shoot the film, is just silly. Most of the celebrated film directors in Hong Kong have co-directed at some time or other. Tony Ching Siu-tung was happy to collaborate with Tsui Hark, as we know – and also to share

---

[1] By the early 2000s, many Hong Kong action directors were working in the West, including Tony Ching Siu-tung, Corey Yuen Kwai, Yuen Cheung-yan and, most famously, Yuen Woo-ping.
[2] A surprising number of actors and crew in the Hong Kong film industry have also directed. Actors, DPs, editors, writers and action choreographers often step into the director's chair.

direction with Wong Jing, Johnnie To Ke-fung, and others.

It's common in the Hong Kong industry for film directors to also be actors, for actors to direct, for writers to be actors, and for some of the really gifted people to have multiple roles (like Sammo Hung, Jackie Chan, Tsui Hark, Eric Tsang, Wu Ma, etc).

TONY CHING SIU-TUNG: FILM CREDITS

Tony Ching Siu-tung's films as director include:

Duel To the Death (1983)
The Witch From Nepal (1986)
A Chinese Ghost Story (1987)
The Terracotta Warrior (1989)
The Swordsman (1990 – co-directed)
A Chinese Ghost Story 2 (1990)
The Raid (1991 – co-directed)
A Chinese Ghost Story 3 (1991)
Swordsman 2 (1992)
Swordsman 3 (1993 – co-directed)
The Heroic Trio (1993, co-directed)
The Executioners (1993, co-directed)
Wonder Seven (1994)
Dr. Wai In "The Scripture With No Words" (1996)
The Longest Day (1997)
Conman In Tokyo (2000)
Naked Weapon (2002)
Belly of the Beast (2003)
An Empress and the Warriors (2008)
The Sorcerer and the White Snake (2011)
Jade Dynasty (2019)

Tony Ching Siu-tung's work as action director/ choreographer includes 84 films up to 2011 (this is in addition to most of the movies he also helmed, where he was the action director, and not forgetting the many TV series that Ching has action directed – see below).

The following is a partial list:

The Fourteen Amazons (1972)
The Rats (1972)
Love and Vengeance (1973)
Shaolin Boxer (1974)
The Tea House (1974)

Kidnap (1974)
Lady of the Law (1975)
Negotiation (1977)
He Who Never Dies (1979)
Monkey Kung Fu (1979)
The Bastard Swordsman (1979)
The Sentimental Swordsman (1979)
Dangerous Encounter - 1st Kind (1980)
The Spooky Bunch (1980)
The Sword (1980)
The Master Strikes (1980)
Gambler's Delight (1981)
Return of the Deadly Blade (1981)
Sword of Justice (1981)
The Story of Woo Viet (1981)
Rolls, Rolls, I Love You (1982)
Once Upon a Rainbow (1982)
Swordsman Adventure (1983)
Twinkle Twinkle Little Star (1983)
Cherie (1984)
Happy Ghost 3 (1986)
Peking Opera Blues (1986)
A Better Tomorrow 2 (1987)
The Eighth Happiness (1988)
I Love Maria (1988)
The Killer (1989)
All About Ah-Long (1989)
The Fun, the Luck and the Tycoon (1990)
Casino Raiders 2 (1991)
Son On the Run (1991)
New Dragon Gate Inn (1992 – co-directed)
Moon Warriors (1992)
Twin Dragons (1992)
Royal Tramp (1992)
Royal Tramp 2 (1992)
Gambling Soul (1992)
Justice, My Foot! (1992)
Lucky Encounter (1992)
Flying Dagger (1993)
Future Cops (1993)
Holy Weapon (1993)
The Mad Monk (1993)
Butterfly and Sword (1993)
City Hunter (1993)
Love On Delivery (1994)
A Chinese Odyssey 1: Pandora's Box (1995)
A Chinese Odyssey 2: Cinderella (1995)

The Stuntwoman (1996)
Warriors of Virtue (1997)
Hong Niang (1998)
The Blacksheep Affair (1998)
The Assassin Swordsman (2000)
The Duel (2000)
My School Mate, the Barbarian (2001)
Invincible (2001)
Shaolin Soccer (2001)
Hero (2002)
Spider-Man (2002 – uncredited)
House of Flying Daggers (2004)
The Curse of the Golden Flower (2006)
Krrish (2006)
In the Name of the King: A Dungeon Siege Tale (2007)
The Warlords (2007)
Dororo (2007)
Legend of Shaolin Kungfu I: Heroes in Troubled Times (2007)
Butterfly Lovers (2008)
Kung Fu Dunk (2008)
The Treasure Hunter (2009)
Future X-Cops (2010)
Just Call Me Nobody (2010)
Legend of Shaolin Kungfu 3: Heroes of the Great Desert (2011)
Krrish 3 (2013)

Tony Ching has been the action director on many television series, including:

The Spirit of the Sword (1978)
It Takes a Thief (1979)
The Roving Swordsman (1979)
Reincarnated (1979)
Reincarnated 2 (1979)
Dynasty (1980)
Dynasty 2 (1980)
Legend of the Condor Heroes (1983)
The Return of the Condor Heroes (1983)
The New Adventures of Chor Lau Heung (1984)
The Duke of Mount Deer (1984)
The Return of Luk Siu Fung (1986)
The New Heaven Sword and Dragon Sabre (1986)
The Storm Riders (a.k.a. *Wind and Cloud*, 2002)
The Storm Riders 2 (a.k.a. *Wind and Cloud 2*, 2004)
The Royal Swordsmen (2005)

It's worth noting a couple of things about the credits of Tony Ching

Siu-tung and other action directors:[3] (1) some sources have Ching as the director, confusing action director with director. (2) The action director does indeed oversee whole sequences of a movie. The director sometimes leaves action scenes (and more) up to them. Also, action direction often includes second unit work. So you could argue that some films are co-directed – especially action movies, where lengthy sections will have been overseen by the action director. (3) And some movies were officially co-directed by Ching, working as a director (often with Tsui Hark). As you can see from the credits and the dates of the movies, co-directing usually occurred in the ultra-busy time of the late 1980s and early-to-mid-1990s, when people were working on four movies simultaneously, and sleeping in their car.

In Tony Ching Siu-tung's case, we know that *New Dragon Gate Inn* ran into trouble, and Ching and Tsui Hark came in to oversee the direction in order to finish the movie (part of which was filmed on location in Mainland China). *The Swordsman* too had problems, with several directors contributing to it to get the whole thing done.

In the West, the division of labour includes stunt co-ordinator, who oversees the stunt team and the stunts, and second unit director, who takes up all of the material that the first or 'A' unit hasn't time to do. In Hong Kong, the action director tends to combine the role of the stunt co-ordinator with that of the second unit director (many of the big name action directors have their own stunt teams – Jackie Chan's guys being the most famous).

How could Tony Ching do so much work in action direction – often several movies in the same year? The answer is the action director or stunt co-ordinator will be hired for short periods, sometimes even a day, to deliver particular effects. Even if they oversee several action sequences, they won't be on board for the whole schedule (for the talky scenes, for instance). Some productions call for a lot more action, of course, which will take longer; but many films hire several action directors (plus assistants). Thus, the action scenes can be filmed simultaneously.

In addition, action teams are often collaborating with the same people on film after film, so they develop a shorthand way of working; they are used to working fast; they often work long hours (without film unions); and they sometimes work on other shows at the same time (having several action directors means that some can be working in the studio, while others are on location).

Tony Ching Siu-tung has provided action direction for Tsui Hark, Johnnie To Ke-fung, John Woo, Wong Jing, Ringo Lam, Zhang Yimou, Peter Chan, Andy Lau, Kevin Chu, and Stephen Chow, among others. That is, practically all of the major filmmakers in China. (Ching has worked many times with a group of directors that include Tsui, Jing, To, Chow, Zhang and Chu. Ching has worked with Jing more than anyone else, except perhaps Tsui). There's no doubt whatsoever that one of the reasons those directors are celebrated by critics and fans around the world is because

---

[3] The 'martial arts director' was a position partly created by director King Hu in the 1960s.

their action sequences were overseen by Ching and his contemporaties.

We might wish, selfishly, that Ching Siu-tung had directed more movies, as with Jackie Chan (13 or so), rather than providing action direction for other filmmakers. However, 22 features as director or co-director, between 1983 and 2019, is a solid career – some of those movies are masterpieces (22 films is more than celebrated directors such as Orson Welles, Andrei Tarkovsky and Luchino Visconti).

TONY CHING SIU-TUNG: BIOGRAPHY

Tony Ching Siu-tung – often known as Tony Ching or as Ching Siu-tung[4] – was born on October 30, 1953, in Anhui, Showhsien province.[5] Ching is a genius of action cinema.[6] No one in the West can touch him, and only his contemporaries among Chinese action choreographers, such as Yuen Woo-ping, Corey Yuen Kwai and Yuen Bun, offer serious competition. Ching is the director of two of the great recent fantasy franchises in Chinese cinema: the *Chinese Ghost Story* series and the *Swordsman* series – two trilogies of pure cinematic bliss.

If these two film trilogies were better-known, Tony Ching Siu-tung would be celebrated like the greats of cinema – Renoir, Rossellini, Mizoguchi, Hawks, and, yes, even Murnau and Griffith. Ching 'demands to be ranked with the most idiosyncratic visionaries in film history', Howard Hampton[7] asserted (*pace The Swordsman 3: The East Is Red*).

Tony Ching Siu-tung[8] has helmed 22 movies (*A Chinese Ghost Story* was only his third feature as director), and has been the action choreographer on some of the very finest action movies of recent times, including *Hero, House of Flying Daggers, The Curse of the Golden Flower, Shaolin Soccer, Moon Warriors, Peking Opera Blues, New Dragon Gate Inn, City Hunter, The Killer, A Better Tomorrow 2* and *Twinkle Twinkle Little Star* (Ching's first action director credits go back to 1972's *The Fourteen Amazons* (his first credit as action director, for a film directed by his father, Ching Gong), and he was an actor in classics such as *Come Drink With Me*, 1966).

Tony Ching won Golden Horse Awards for *New Dragon Gate Inn* and *Shaolin Soccer*, Hong Kong Film Awards for *The Witch From Nepal, The*

---

4 As usual in China, there are many variants on his name, including: Xiaodong Cheng, Cheng Sao Tung, Ching Ting Yee, Cheng Bao-shan, Cheng Hsiao-tung and Shao-Tung Cheng.
  The names in Chinese cinema are confusing: there are at least two and often more for each person: a Chinese name, and an Angelicized name. Further, names in Cantonese and Mandarin are different. There is also some confusion about first names and surnames or family names – names're often printed with the surname first. And a single vowel change can mean a different name: Chang or Cheng, for example. So it's easy to be confused by the many Wongs, Laus, Leungs, Cheungs and Yuens!
5 Other sources say it was Hong Kong.
6 'The world's greatest wire-rig wizard', said Lisa Morton (LM, 88).
7 Quoted in F. Dannen, 338.
8 Cheng Xiaodong in pinyin.

Swordsman and *Hero,* as well as awards for *A Chinese Ghost Story*.

Ching Siu-tung has returned to work in television from time to time. For ex, in 2002 and 2004, he was the action choreographer on the long-running series *The Storm Riders,* also known as *Cloud and Wind.* This Taiwanese production of 45 episodes was based on a comic (known in China as *manhua*) by Ma Wing-shing called *Fung Wan.*

Tony Ching Siu-tung's father is Ching Gong (b. April 7, 1924, also known as Cheng Kang), a writer and director at Shaw Brothers. Ching senior was directing Cantonese films occasionally from 1951 onwards, filmed 2nd unit for Shaws in the 1960s, became a full director in 1967, and his output (of some 30 titles) includes many swordplay movies. He was very active in the 1950s-1970s as a writer – he's known for films such as *The Magnificent Swordsman* (1968) and *The Fourteen Amazons* (1972). His last film as director was *Gambling Soul* (1992).

Ching junior worked at Shaws as a stuntman,[9] sometimes on his Dad's movies; he grew up on film sets. Later, Ching acted as action director on several of his father's films. (Unfortunately, as with so many Hong Kong movies, many of them are not widely available).

Ching Gong was a writer for many years before directing – he has an impressive list of credits. However, the desire to write didn't transfer to his son – Ching has very few writing credits.

Tony Ching trained for seven years in Peking Opera and in *kung fu* in the Northern Style, at the East Drama School, run by Tang Ti.

✳

Sidenote on the Shaws: the Shaw Brothers Studio at Clearwater Bay in Hong Kong was launched in 1957 by Sir Run Run Shaw (Shao Yifu). Dubbed 'Movie Town', the 49-acre complex included eleven sound stages, fifteen standing sets on the backlot (featuring old Chinese settings), post-production, dubbing and editing facilities, print laboratories, dormitories and apartments for the casts and crews, and its own film school. (Run Run Shaw was in Singapore before this, overseeing distribution and acquiring properties. He came to Canton to take over the business from his brother, Runde).

Shaw Brothers kept players and talent on contracts, as in the Hollywood system (some 1700 workers).[10] The pay was famously low. Altho' the Hong Kong operation was regarded as Shaw Brothers, each brother oversaw companies within the empire. Shaws wasn't just a production facility/ studio, it had a distribution network.

Run Run Shaw spent HK $800,000 (= US $103,000) per movie; they were filmed in colour and in widescreen (Shawscope). Shaw was a canny and energetic businessman. He made deals with overseas producers, such as Italian producers, and the British Hammer studio (a famous investment was $7.5 million for foreign rights in the Warner Brothers/ Tandem/ Ladd Company movie *Blade Runner*, 1982).

✳

---

[9] As Ching was small, he sometimes doubled for women.
[10] At its height, the Shaw Brothers operation had 1,500 actors and 2,000 staff, an 80,000 wardrobe dept, a drama school (of 120 students), and in-house magazines.

One of Tony Ching Siu-tung's specialities is wire-work (there is plenty in the *Chinese Ghost Story* series); another is swordplay. Ching can fly actors and stunties with a blissful disregard for anything as everyday as gravity. The speed, invention, spontaneity, timing, rhythm, and acrobatic dynamism of Ching's action scenes are truly marvellous. Also worth remarking upon is the visual style of Ching's films: they have a highly romantic, luxurious look, with particular attention to art direction, costumes and textures. His films exploit props and the physical environment to a striking degree (this is true of many Hong Kong action movies). But Ching seems to go further than anyone else in evoking mystery, beauty and romance. Ching is an all-round filmmaker, and his mark is everywhere in his movies. Even amongst many similar films in Hong Kong cinema, Ching's stand out. Ching has said that entertainment is the highest priority for him as a filmmaker – like Tsui Hark, he is a supreme example of the Filmmaker As Showman.

Tony Ching Siu-tung is also a master of visual effects – no doubt he learnt plenty from Tsui Hark and Film Workshop, but visual effects and practical effects are a key ingredient in the Chingian style of filmmaking. If there's a cinematic trick available, Ching will use it. 'I like being unconventional', he remarked.

The movies of Ching Siu-tung foreground the tricks and visual effects of cinema; Western filmmakers who also use this approach include: Orson Welles, Jean Cocteau, Walerian Borowczyk, Sergei Paradjanov, Tim Burton, Vincente Minnelli, Powell & Pressburger, Ken Russell and Francis Coppola. Films of Ching's such as *A Chinese Ghost Story* are filled with visual effects (the influence of producer Tsui Hark is clear in this production).

Only in Hong Kong has the kind of action choreography delivered by Tony Ching and his contemporaries been possible. Nowhere else on this planet has action direction this complicated, this fast, this imaginative and this entertaining, using wires, rigs, harnesses, pulleys, cranes and ropes, been seen in movies.

Ching Siu-tung was promoted to martial arts coordinator in movies in the '70s, and worked in television (at Commercial Television) as a martial arts coordinator (at the invitation of Anthony Leung). Ching was the chief martial arts adviser on the 1979 TV series *Meteor, Butterfly, Sword*. He worked for Rediffusion Television on TV series such as *The Spirit of the Sword* (1978), *It Takes a Thief* (1979), *The Roving Swordsman* (1979), *Reincarnated* (1979), *Reincarnated 2* (1979), *Dynasty* (1980) and *Dynasty 2* (1980).

Tony Ching continued to work in television throughout the 1980s, including Hong Kong Television Broadcast series such as: *Legend of the Condor Heroes* (1983), *The Return of the Condor Heroes* (1983), *The New Adventures of Chor Lau Heung* (1984), *The Duke of Mount Deer* (1984), *The Return of Luk Siu Fung* (1986) and *The New Heaven Sword and Dragon Sabre* (1986). This extensive work in television partly explains the gap of three years between the feature productions *Duel To the Death* and *The*

Witch From Nepal.

Tony Ching's first full-length, theatrical film as director was *Duel To the Death* (1983), which was, of course, a *wuxia pian*. Ching's first collaboration with Tsui Hark on a feature film was *Dangerous Encounter – 1st Kind* in 1980, tho' they had already worked together in television.

Tony Ching has moved into North American movies (with *Belly of the Beast* (2003), a Steven Seagal actioner), worked uncredited on *Spider-man* (2002), has choreographed the Indian superhero movie *Krrish* (2006), and the sequels, produced the pop video *L'Âme-Stram-Gram* (1999) for French pop star Mylène Farmer, and contributed to the 2008 Beijing Olympics (at the invitation of director Zhang Yimou).

Tony Ching has been an actor many times, taking lead roles in *Monkey Kung Fu* (1979) and *The Master Strikes* (1980). Ching launched his own production company in 1993, China Entertainment.

Tony Ching Siu-tung's directing credits (22 features up to 2019) include *Dr Wai, The Sorcerer and the White Snake, Jade Dynasty, Wonder Seven, An Empress and the Warriors, Belly of the Beast, The Terracotta Warrior, The Raid* (co-directed), *The Witch From Nepal* and *The Executioners.* Ching's credits as action director (84 films up to 2011!) include *Butterfly Lovers, The Warlords, Shaolin Soccer, Invincible, In the Name of the King, Holy Weapon, Spider-man, Moon Warriors*, the *Royal Tramp* films (sometimes credited with co-direction), *Peking Opera Blues, Krrish, Butterfly and Sword* (sometimes credited with co-direction), *Bloodmoon, Hero, House of Flying Daggers, The Curse of the Golden Flower, The Royal Swordsmen* (TV series), *The Duel, Chinese Odyssey, Kung Fu Dunk, City Hunter, Twin Dragons, Future Cops, The Killer, A Better Tomorrow 2, The Storm Riders* (a.k.a. *Cloud and Wind*, TV series, 2002/ 2004), and *Twinkle Twinkle Little Star.*

Altho' John Woo, Yuen Woo-ping and Tsui Hark receive many of the accolades from film critics (and fans) for their depiction of action on screen, I am struck with awe at the imagination and magnificence of Tony Ching Siu-tung's work. He is the equal of Tsui, Woo, Yuen *et al*, and in some respects he out-does them (he has also of course worked as an action choreographer for all of the big names in Hong Kong action cinema). For action with a high fantasy component, Ching can't be beat – look at his work in *Hero* or *The House of Flying Daggers* or *Moon Warriors*, for instance. (And let's remember that Ching worked as action director for many Hong Kong directors, including John Woo: one of the reasons that the *Better Tomorrow* movies or *The Killer* are so good is because it's Ching choreographing the action. And it's often the action that critics rave about in those Woo-helmed movies).

Producer Terence Chang said that Tsui Hark and Tony Ching Siu-tung complemented each other: while Tsui was enamoured of the historical pictures from the Shaw Brothers, Ching actually worked on them: 'they complemented each other and were tied together by their shared romantic vision', Chang remarked.

Indeed – of all of Tsui Hark's many, many creative collaborations, the ones with Tony Ching Siu-tung are among the most productive: they seem to have sparked each other to greater imaginative heights, as evinced by the *Chinese Ghost Story* series and the *Swordsman* series (both made in the busy late 1980s/ early 1990s period).

Jeff Yang noted that Tony Ching Siu-tung was about the only director able to work with Tsui Hark consistently, maybe because he got along with Tsui, or because he was happy to let Tsui take all of the glory (2003, 97). Also, directors in Hong Kong are happy to share director credits – most of the major directors have done it.

Maybe Tony Ching Siu-tung was able to accommodate Tsui Hark and his tendency to wade in heavy and strong to a film project and not get freaked out by it. Maybe Ching realized that the movies they were producing were extraordinary (so a bit of aggro didn't matter, and aggro doesn't last anyway). Maybe Ching was easy-going enough (where other filmmakers in this period found it just too difficult to work with Tsui, and some walked out).

Because Tony Ching Siu-tung clearly threw himself 100% into the three *Chinese Ghost Story* movies (and the *Swordsman* movies). These are film productions that literally *roar* with fire and energy and humour and action and sweetness and tenderness and mind-boggling eccentricity. There's *so much* energy on screen, these movies are like a conflagration.

As a director, Ching Siu-tung's career has been a tad uneven: low-points include *Naked Weapon* and *Belly of the Beast*, two mean-spirited films that Ching directed which were not worthy of his talents. However, in 2002 and 2003 Ching also action directed two sublime examples of action cinema: *Hero* and *House of Flying Daggers* (plus the great comedy *Shaolin Soccer*, and the TV series *The Storm Riders*). Soon after that, Ching provided the action direction for *Krrish* and *The Curse of the Golden Flower* (both 2006), and took up the directing reins in 2008 for his masterpiece *An Empress and the Warriors*.

PEKING OPERA.

Tony Ching trained in Peking Opera, a breeding ground for many future Hong Kong and Chinese stars. Peking Opera is known as *jingju* = theatre of the capital. The four performance skills in Peking Opera are *da* (acrobatics and martial skills), *chang* (singing), *nian* (reciting) and *zuo* (acting).

In Chinese Opera, as in many theatrical traditions, men play women's roles (so that only men're on stage). Yam Kin-fai and Pak Suet-sin, for instance, played across the gender divide in the Opera movies of the 1950s and 1960s. In Cantonese Opera, the fighting instructor was called *longhu* (= Dragon-Tiger Master).

The Peking Opera approach to entertainment was characterized thus by Bey Logan:

> extravagant costumes, bright full-face makeup, Olympic-class gymnastics, and both weapon and empty-handed combat, as well as a

rich tradition of character, music and drama. (9)

Beijing Opera is the most well-known form of Chinese Opera, but it's not the only one. There are 100s of Opera styles, including Cantonese Opera. Acrobatics, extravagant costumes, make-up, singing, music, and stylized gestures constitute the performance style. Most of the performers have traditionally been men. The heyday of Chinese Opera was the 1930s. Following its decline in the 1960s and 1970s, performers moved into the film industry.

Peking Opera's most famous academy was the one run by Sifu Yu Jim Yuen in Hong Kong, the stern taskmaster who oversaw the performance troupe that included Jackie Chan, Sammo Hung, Yuen Biao, Yuen Tak, Yuen Wah, Yuen Bun and Yuen Kwai (Corey Yuen). They were known as the Seven Fortunes (tho' there were fourteen of them). Their upbringing at the academy was immortalized in the 1988 movie *Painted Faces* (with Hung playing the *sifu*). As Hung, Chan, Biao and others have often remarked, the regime overseen by Yu was so harsh, no one would believe them! (Even though in the *Painted Faces* movie what the boys have to undergo is pretty tough).

HONG KONG CINEMA IN CRITICISM.

The critical response to Hong Kong cinema in recent years tends to celebrate the same movies, and the same filmmakers are enshrined by the critical academy: Tsui Hark, John Woo, Yuen Woo-ping, Wong kar-wai, Johnny To, Lau Kar-leung, Peter Chan, Stanley Kwan, Corey Yuen Kwai, Sammo Hung, Ronny Yu, Ann Mui, Ringo Lam, and of course Jackie Chan. Tony Ching Siu-tung is part of that list.

The same actors are exalted: Jackie Chan, Jet Li, Chow Yun-fat, Tony Leung, Andy Lau, Leslie Cheung, Sammo Hung, Yuen Biao, Donnie Yen, Stephen Chow, Leon Lai, Jacky Cheung, Simon Lam, Joey Wong, Zhao Wenzhou, Zhao Wei, Chingmy Yau, Anita Mui, Michelle Yeoh, Maggie Cheung, Brigitte Lin, Michelle Reiss, Carrie Ng, Cherie Chung, Rosamund Kwan, Sally Yeh and Zhang Ziyi.

The much-discussed Hong Kong movies include the *Once Upon a Time In China* series, the *Police Story* series, the *Project A* films, the *Armor of God* films, the *Better Tomorrow* series, the *Stormriders* series, the *Fong Sai-yuk/ Legend* series, the *Lucky Stars* series, the *Bride With White Hair* series, the *On Fire* series, *Rouge, Mr Vampire, Rumble In the Bronx, Zu: Warriors From the Magic Mountain, Peking Opera Blues, Painted Faces, Infernal Affairs, Dragons Forever, Drunken Master, Snake In Eagle's Shadow, Iron Monkey, Moon Warriors, The Spooky Bunch, Royal Tramp, Bullet In the Head, The Killer, Hard-Boiled, God of Gamblers, Chungking Express, Ashes of Time, Aces Go Places, Wicked City, City Hunter, Naked Killer, Sex and Zen*, etc. And of course every critic also cites the Bruce Lee movies, and the Shaw Brothers classics.

Tony Ching has several movies that're part of that list: the *Swordsman* series and the *Chinese Ghost Story* series; he has worked on many classics directed by others, too: *New Dragon Gate Inn, Moon Warriors, A Better Tomororw 2, Peking Opera Blues* and *The Killer.*

You try finding a study of Chinese cinema or Hong Kong cinema between 1980 and today that *doesn't* mention *any* of the above movies or directors or actors! So it's a narrow group of film classics, in short.

REMAKES AND UPDATES.

Much of Ching Siu-tung's cinema comprises updating and remaking previous movies and stories. Hong Kong filmmakers know their history, and how their industry is constantly recycling and updating earlier movies. As Ching notes, you have to be contemporary, you can't be out of date. As an action director, Ching has worked on many remakes and updates of earlier films: *A Better Tomorrow* was a remake of *Story of a Discharged Prisoner* (a.k.a. *True Colors of a Hero,* 1967*), New Dragon Gate Inn* updated the King Hu-helmed movie of 1967, and *The Warlords* was a remake of *The Blood Brothers* (1973).

In thriving film cultures, like France, Japan, Korea or the U.S.A., it is completely expected and normal to remake movies and stories all the time. *New actors in old stories* is one of the definitions of the Hollywood movie machine in the glory days of the 1930s thru 1960s, but the phrase still sums up a large proportion of the output of any flourishing filmmaking centre. Often, the remakes and updates are simply old stories dressed up in new clothes, with some new gimmicks to help sell them (such as 3-D, or visual effects, or a postmodern spin on an old chestnut).

CHING SIU-TUNG AND TELEVISION.

Television nurtured the New Wave filmmakers in Hong Kong – becoming something like a Shaolin Temple for cinéastes, as critic Law Kar put it. They worked at stations such as C.T.V. (Commercial Television), R.T.H.K. (Radio Television Hong Kong) and T.V.B.[11] (Hong Kong Television Broadcast, Ltd.). Selina Chow, a TV executive, was instrumental in hiring the 'New Wave' filmmakers in television.[12] They were also a film school generation: the New Wave directors studied at film schools abroad partly because they didn't really exist in Asia (the Chinese State film school, Beijing Film Academy, didn't re-open until 1978).

Ching Siu-tung worked a good deal in television, from the 1970s onwards. Before he helmed his first feature, *Duel To the Death* in 1983, Ching had already been an action director for TV shows such as *The Spirit of the Sword* (1978), *It Takes a Thief* (1979), *The Roving Swordsman* (1979), *Reincarnated* (1979), *Reincarnated 2* (1979), *Meteor, Butterfly, Sword* (1979), *Dynasty* (1980) and *Dynasty 2* (1980). Ching returned to television production periodically – in 2002 and 2004, for example, Ching action directed the *Storm Riiders* TV series (a.k.a. *Wind and Cloud*).

---

[11] T.V.B. was the television arm of Shaws.
[12] Lisa Morton, 221.

THE HONG KONG NEW WAVE.

Ching Siu-tung was not one of the New Wave of Hong Kong filmmakers who went to film school overseas – instead, Ching grew up in the film industry: his father Ching Gong was a film director at Shaws. However, Ching worked on many of the New Wave productions – three in 1980, for example: *The Sword, Dangerous Encounter* and *The Spooky Bunch*.

Many of the Chinese New Wave filmmakers were film school graduates: Ann Hui and Yim Ho studied in London; Tsui Hark in Austin, Texas; and Ringo Lam in Toronto (York University). They studied in the West, or in Western-style institutions in Hong Kong. They could speak English with critics, which no doubt helped, because they'd spent time in the West. And they were familiar with the art film traditions of Europe and the U.S.A.

Following film school, they went to work in television. (Hui, Ho and Tsui were part of the first wave of the New Wave, along with Allan Fong, Patrick Tam, Kirk Wong, and Tony Ching Siu-tung); the second wave included Stanley Kwan, Alex Law, Clara Law, Cheung Yuen-ting, Jacob Cheung, Wong Kar-wai, and Eddie Fong.

The Hong Kong New Wave did not have a style or an approach: it took on aspects of youth: 'school, sex, drugs and other travails of growing up in a materialistic society, misunderstood by parents and adults in authority', according to Stephen Teo (1997, 156).

It was no surprise that many of the first films of the Hong Kong New Wave were thrillers or crime stories – because they are a staple of Hong Kong cinema, and of cinemas the world over, because they tend to be cheap to make, because the genre was versatile, and because a huge proportion of source material was in the crime or thriller genre.

For Stephen Teo, the two strands of the Hong Kong New Wave cinema – realism and genre conventions – developed towards the latter: the New Wavers started out tackling realism but lent towards genre filmmaking (1997, 149). The forms and conventions of genres were updated for modern audiences in the 1980s. (The first official, Hong Kong New Wave film was *The Extras* (1978), but the unofficial film that launched it, according to Cheuk Pak-tong, was *Jumping Ash* (1976). In 1979, some of the first New Wave films included *The Secrets* (dir. Ann Hui), *The Butterfly Murders* (dir. Tsui Hark), *The System* (dir. Peter Yung) and *Cops and Robbers* (dir. Alex Cheung)). By contrast, Ching Siu-tung's first film as director was the high fantasy swordplay movie *Duel To the Death* in 1983.

At the height of the 1990s New Wave, actors and crew were commonly rushing from one movie set to another. Andy Lau Tak-wah slept in his car while filming a movie a month in 1991, and according to rumour making four movies in four locations at the same time. (Chinese filmmakers became geniuses at stretching footage of actors who could only give them a day or so, by using doubles, re-arranging scripts, focussing on reaction shots, etc).

You'll see the same actors and directors in the New Wave of Hong Kong and Chinese cinema, continuing up to the present day. The actors include: Jet Li, Jackie Chan, Brigitte Lin, Tony Leung, Leslie Cheung, Michelle Yeoh Chu-kheng, Zhao Wei, Donnie Yen, Maggie Cheung, Jacky Cheung, Zhang Ziyi, Yuen Biao, Chow Yun-fat, Josephine Siao, Stephen Chow, Gong Li, Rosamund Kwan, Zhao Wenzhou, Kent Cheng, and Xiong Xin-xin.

And directors such as Tsui Hark, Ronny Yu, Ringo Lam, King Hu, Sammo Hung, Zhang Yimou, Ann Hui, Wong Jing, Yuen Woo-ping, Wong Kar-wai, Stanley Tong and John Woo. Tony Ching Siu-tung is part of that group.

The second wave of Hong Kong filmmakers occurred in the mid-1980s, and included filmmakers such as Stanley Kwan (*Rouge, The Actress*), Wong Kar-wai (*Ashes of Time, Chungking Express*), Clara Law (*The Reincarnation of Golden Lotus*), Mabel Cheung (*An Autumn's Tale*), Lawrence Ah Mon (*Gangs, Queen of Temple Street*), Alex Law (*Painted Faces*), Eddie Fong, and Jacob Cheung.

✷

Hong Kong is a city of seven million or so. The filmmaking community is small: everybody knows or has heard of everyone else. Over its history, the cast and crew of Hong Kong movies would've met many times at the Shaw Brothers' studios at Clearwater Bay, or the Golden Harvest studios in Diamond Hill, or the television studios at Hong Kong Television Broadcast, Ltd. They would visit the same bars and restaurants. Some American filmmakers prefer to shoot outside of L.A., because if you film in Tinseltown everybody knows what you're doing. No chance of avoiding that in Hong Kong!

You'll see the same downtown areas of Hong Kong, the same harbour fronts, the same strips of forest or beaches, and the same standing sets of 19th century China, in movie after movie. (And, with the problems of obtaining film permits, shooting on location on the streets often means guerilla-style filmmaking, which Hong Kong crews are experts at).

Ching Siu-tung on set.

Making Jade Dynasty (2019), this page and over.

小战战与河水结下了深刻的革命友谊

[是他抢我的棍子]

2

ASPECTS OF THE CINEMA OF TONY CHING SIU-TUNG

'MORE POWER!': SOME OF TONY CHING SIU-TUNG'S MOTIFS

Tony Ching Siu-tung's on-set mantra is, 'more power, more power!' Among the many motifs and techniques in Ching's style of action direction are:

• an emphasis on the beauty and flow of bodies in motion (Tony Ching Siu-tung is probably the most painterly of Hong Kong action directors);

• fluttering, flapping robes, banners and flags (fans are continually blowing on a Ching set);

• mass battles – chaotic movement everywhere; typically, someone will bounce on a hidden trampoline across the camera;

• extremely rapid swordplay accompanied by jumps and acrobatic spins, and often moving across the ground, covered in tracking shots;

• the lone swordsman entering the fray, weapon extended, like Superman;

• groups of figures lowered on wires – it might be the heroes arriving at a scene, or henchmen (*Krrish*), or some ghoulish characters (as in *A Chinese Ghost Story*);

• water explosions – multiple fountains of water from oil barrels, often erupting behind a magician (as in the *Chinese Ghost Story* series, *Moon Warriors*, the *Swordsman* films and *Royal Tramp 2*);

• long distance airborne travel – a palanquin complete with footmen hurtling thru the tree-tops at speed;

• ærial flight gags – ninjas[1] flying on kites;

• visual effects – these are everywhere in Tony Ching Siu-tung's cinema, combined with action;

• charas (often ninja) diving into frame from either side of a rapidly-tracking camera;

• exiting a scene by soaring upwards and crashing thru a roof;

• hidden attacks from high above, sword pointing down;

---
[1] Bey Logan calls the ninjas that regularly pop up in the films of Tony Ching 'Chinjas'.

- horror movie gags (giant tongues);
- gross-out gags – people or horses[2] split apart; people exploding in a flurry of blood and rags;
- massive gags and stunts – disintegrating wooden platforms, flying logs, collapsing buildings, crazy monsters, enormous explosions.

ELEMENTS OF CHING SIU-TUNG'S CINEMA

The 22 films directed (and co-directed) by Ching Siu-tung (up to 2019) feature the following elements:

- They all have Chinese casts (with one or two exceptions).
- They all use Hong Kong and Chinese crews.
- They are all set in Asia, and usually in China or Hong Kong, with one or two overseas locations.
- They are all Chinese stories (with one or two exceptions).
- They are all produced in China (with the odd overseas trip).
- They draw heavily on Chinese tradition and history.
- About half can be classed as swordplay movies (or *wuxia pian*). The rest are thrillers or action-adventures.
- Two-thirds are historical movies; one third are contemporary-set.
- Comedy is a significant element in at least half of the films.
- All of the films climax with a giant action scene.
- Ching Siu-tung has action director credits on all of them.

These elements speak for themselves: most of Ching Siu-tung's films have been about China, set in China, with Chinese stories featuring Chinese characters, using Chinese crews and casts, and two-thirds have been historical movies.

ASPECTS OF THE CINEMA OF TONY CHING SIU-TUNG

Tony Ching Siu-tung told the Hong Kong Film Directors' Guild:

> I like beautiful, romantic things, and have an almost extreme and idealized sense of perfectionism regarding the films I make, and strive to achieve the kind of poeticism found in traditional Chinese paintings.

---

[2] If you love horses and don't like to see them harmed – even if you know it's movie fakery – don't watch Hong Kong action movies! Horses are punched and wrestled to the ground (*An Empress and the Warriors*), decapitated (*Burning Paradise*), pushed down steep slopes (*Seven Swords*), and sliced in two (Tony Ching Siu-tung's films).

Keep those things in mind when considering Tony Ching Siu-tung's cinema: romance, idealization, perfection, painting and poetry. (And remember, too, that Ching trained in Peking Opera for 7 years).

Altho' Ching Siu-tung is known as an action director and a film director who showcases action, romance, comedy and a painterly vision are also key elements of his cinema. For instance, his first big hit movie was a romance (*A Chinese Ghost Story*), and romance was an important ingredient in the *Swordsman* films, in *The Terracotta Warrior* and more recent films, such as *An Empress and the Warriors* (which features a lengthy romantic idyll).

Tony Ching Siu-tung said he liked to try new ways of approaching storytelling, and he enjoyed taking on fantasy forms. Why? – 'Because I'm not a normal person. I think it's fun to shoot something different, something unusual'.

When he was asked what the secret was of being a good action director, Tony Ching Siu-tung replied:

The secret is to stay young. Your ideas can't age with you – although we're getting older, what we film has to feel young. It's not okay to be outdated.

Tsui Hark on action:

Action is not just by itself; action always comes with a story, it also comes with a style, it comes with extra information about what the director wants to show to the audience. These sorts of things are always with me. (2011)

Tony Leung Siu-hung noted that action choreographers have to imprint their style on a scene:

All comes from your mind, your imagination. You then have to share it with your assistant. It's the same with Tony Ching Siu-tung; after he's finished working on a choreographed scene, it's eventually Ching Siu-tung's imagination which appears at the end. (A. Lanuque, 2006)

When he's directing, Tony Ching Siu-tung is amongst the actors and crew, not hiding in a video village off to one side. He is interacting directly with the cast, including all of the principals, showing them how to perform the action, often at a micro, beat-by-beat level. (That's partly because an action director can't hide behind a bank of monitors and assistant directors, they have to be in the thick of things). Ching also operates the camera himself, so we are often seeing Ching's own compositions and camera moves in his films.

One of Tony Ching's early assistants, Tony Leung Siu-hung, remarked: 'I really admire some of his creations. He's got no limitations! He really knows how to use camera angles and camera movement' (A. Lanuque, 2006).

One of the hallmarks of Tony Ching Siu-tung's form of action cinema is excessive, fantastical violence, action so quick, intense and extreme it borders on the comical. Such as Ching's penchant for warriors being ripped in half by swords in mid-air, or bodies being sliced apart from head to toe and the two halves falling away. In a Ching swordplay flick, victims are decapitated with a single swish of the blade and the heads spin thru the air.[3] It all happens so rapidly, and without showers of blood, it seems 'unrealistic'. But how can you test 'realism'? – like, when was the last time you saw a warrior in full battle armour being torn to pieces by a slashing swordsman – while both of them were in mid-air, at night, in a forest?

Wire-work: the signature image of Tony Ching Siu-tung's cinema is a swordsman flying through the air, sword arm extended, robes fluttering in the breeze. Ching has several motifs in his wire-work which recur: one is flying several characters at the same time, in groups (a great example occurs in the *Chinese Ghost Story* movies. What you don't see are forty guys off-stage hauling on the ropes and cables,[4] and the enormous cranes).[5] Another is a gentle, romantic flight over a long distance (often it's two lovers, embracing and smiling at each other. Sometimes they're on horseback). Another is the rapid exit from a interior scene by zooming upwards, smashing through the roof. When a swordsman enters or exits a scene of combat, they always spin quickly in the air, and also dive and tumble (these moves are very Peking Opera-ish, emulating the way that performers make their entrance on stage. A flashy entrance is a big deal in Peking Opera). Halfway thru a sword fight, a warrior will disappear – then they materialize far above the opponent, and descend swiftly, sword arm stretched out.

Inanimate objects: the wire-work in Hong Kong action movies is puppeteering the environment extensively: walls topple, tables spin, benches are smashed apart, ladders, columns and logs fly thru the air as weapons, and entire buildings collapse. In a Hong Kong action flick, the whole environment can come alive. Special wire-work in Tony Ching Siu-tung's output includes his penchant for very extravagant deaths – victims are torn apart by sword slices or magic.

While we're celebrating the outrageous stunts and wire-work of Hong Kong action directors, we must also remember that they have whole teams of very clever engineers and talented craftsmen who can build all of those rigs, cable systems, scaffolding, cranes and all the rest (and a bunch of burly guys to hang into the wires and the ropes). Stunt gags require plenty of prep work – building breakaway sets or props, for ex, or manœuvring the cranes into the right position. It's one thing you *don't* see in any 'making of' documentaries – just how those complex rigs work. (Partly, perhaps, because sometimes film crews like to keep one or two tricks of the trade secret).

Ninjas! No other film director, in the West, the East, the North, the South – or on Mars – has been so crazy about ninjas and putting them on

---

[3] Pre-dating *Sleepy Hollow* (1999) by many years.
[4] It requires several people to fly one actor.
[5] Photos or detailed descriptions of just how Ching and his crews achieve their effects are hard to find – because they want to keep it secret.

film (outside of Japanese *anime*). Tony Ching just adores those mysterious, black-clad warriors of stealth and cunning. If there's a chance to include some tumbling, running, super-soldiers in a scene, Ching will take it. (And Ching is especially fond of inventing all sorts of incredible gags for the *shinobi* to perform). It's a pity, perhaps, that Ching hasn't (yet) directed a whole movie about *shinobi*. (If you were going to produce a live-action version of a Japanese ninja tale, such as *Naruto,* Ching is definitely your man).

One of Tony Ching's talents is to make actresses look fantastic when they're in action. Hong Kong cinema has a long tradition of female fighters, but most of the actresses in Ching's films (and others of the 1970s through 2010s) are not professional or trained martial artists (and neither are most of the men). But Ching can make them look incredible: Maggie Cheung, Anita Mui, Sharla Cheung, Fennie Yuen, Zhang Ziyi, Kelly Chen, Michelle Reiss, Brigitte Lin, Flora Cheung, Meng Meiqi and Tang Yixin.

Although the Hong Kong film business is male-oriented and masculinist, like all film centres around the world, some of the movies of Tony Ching and his contemporaries have been written by women. Sandy Shaw Lai-king, for instance, wrote *The Heroic Trio, The Executioners* and *Dr Wai* (Shaw's other credits include *Once a Cop, My Father Is a Hero, The Mad Monk, Justice, My Foot!, Twinkle Twinkle Little Star* and *It Runs In the Family.* Some of those movies were directed by or starred John Woo and Stephen Chow).

Many of the movies that Tony Ching works on are cast young – film producers often have an eye on attracting a young audience. Being young, the actors don't have much – or any – experience with complicated stunts, or doing wire-work, or co-operating with visual effects (effects that are created in front of the camera or added later in post-production).

Thus, one of Tony Ching's jobs on any new movie production is training – to teach the young actors how to work with cables and rigs and visual effects. (This is a key reason why some film directors like to work with the same people, who're often veterans of many movies, precisely because they *don't* have to go through the explanations and training each time. But others welcome it).

If you look at the movies that Tony Ching has chosen to do as an action choreographer, you can see that he is one of those people who thrives on new challenges and working with young people. As he says, films and filmmakers have to stay up to date.

All of Ching Siu-tung's movies as director, and most of those as action director, climax with a giant battle. No matter what the movie has been about, the ending is always a massive sequence of incredible action.

Tony Ching Siu-tung doesn't employ slow motion nearly as much as some of his contemporaries. And some of the directors he's worked for as an action choreographer over-use slo-mo, which spoils the sequences he's devised. (However, having said that, I've just watched the group of movies made in the early 2000s again – *Invincible, Hero, Naked Weapon* and *Belly of the Beast* – which do employ a good proportion of slo-mo per fight).

Many Chinese action movies employ slow motion, and also step-motion. Indeed, step-motion (a.k.a. step-printed film) occurs just as much as slow motion. True slow motion is of course filmed on the set, with the camera running at higher speeds (48 frames per second or 96 f.p.s. being typical speeds). But step-motion is created after the fact, in the editing room and by optically treating the celluloid in the processing lab (where you can also select different kinds of step-motion). Sometimes Chinese action movies play whole beats of an action scene in step-motion, but with heightened sound effects (and usually a big music cue). Incidentally, Tony Ching often films action scenes slightly under-cranked (at 22 f.p.s.), to give them an extra ziiip.

Let's not forget, either, that *comedy* and *humour is absolutely fundamental* to the action direction of Tony Ching Siu-tung. Oh yes, Ching is not a dour, old curmudgeon who never cracks a smile, who never allows a smidgen of humour to infect movies with wall-to-wall grimness and frowningness.

In fact, many of Tony Ching Siu-tung's finest works in action are comedies, or feature comedy as a key ingredient, like *Shaolin Soccer*, *A Chinese Ghost Story*, *City Hunter*, *Krrish*, *Jade Dynasty* and *Heroic Trio*. And his two famous series – the *Swordsman* series and *Chinese Ghost Story* series – are stuffed with humour. Ching has worked many times with comedy directors and actors such as Wong Jing and Stephen Chow.

For some critics, the emphasis in the marketing of Chinese and Hong Kong movies in the West on action, violence, energy and weirdness has put it back into a pigeon-hole, which ignores many other kinds of cinema coming out of Hong Kong, Shanghai or Beijing.

Comedy is certainly one of the staple (and lucrative) genres of Hong Kong cinema, often ignored or derided by Western critics. For instance, between 1950 and 1970, 25% of films from Canton were comedies (of the 3,000 films produced). An industry like Hong Kong only produces that many comedy movies if it knows they are going to find an audience. And they do.

In the West, in the U.S.A., martial arts films, action films and art films are the biggest financial successes (and with the film critics), but in Hong Kong, it's *comedies* that have ruled the local box office. Nine out of the ten bestsellers in the 1980s and 1990s in Canton and Taiwan were comedies. Often they are combined with other genres: vampire comedies, kung fu/ martial arts comedies, cookery comedies, gambling comedies, historical comedies, detective/ thriller comedies, etc. (But comedies, as we know, are hampered by problems of translation, dubbing, and cultural specificity. So that giant stars in Asia like Stephen Chow or Michael Hui are still largely unknown in the West. Instead of Adam Sandler or Ben Stiller, try some Stephen Chow for a change).

✺

Tony Ching Siu-tung is not a screenwriter, other people write the scripts that he directs (Ching has only two credits as screenwriter – *Duel*

To the Death and *Wonder Seven*). He is also not a film producer (he has only 4 producer credits). Ching comes to cinema from the practical, organizational side of things, graduating from acting and stuntwork to action choreography and direction.

Tony Ching is thus not an *auteur*, in the manner of filmmakers who write and direct (and also produce) their own material. Much of the time, Ching is a director for hire, someone who's offered scripts and projects – which's how most directors operate (the proportion of film directors who write their own material *and* originate it *and* it's not based on any existing property is *very* small).

Yet Tony Ching Siu-tung's stamp is all over the movies he directs, and his action choreography is instantly recognizable when he works on other productions (especially his style of fantastical swordplay). Certainly, Ching is as natural a filmmaker as any in film history. And tho' not an *auteur* with issues he explores in film after film, he does have recurring themes and motifs. Romance is uppermost, as is action. If something can be expressed in choreography (not always action or military choreography), Ching will try it. This is the Peking Opera form of filmmaking, where gesture and movement, alongside costume and make-up, do the storytelling. In Peking Opera, as soon as an actor steps onto the stage, the audience knows who they are by their clothes, accessories and make-up – and their movement and gestures. Applied to movies, the Peking Opera approach is all over Hong Kong cinema (and Chinese cinema), and informs much of Ching's work (he trained in it for seven years).

Tony Ching Siu-tung is not known for being a firebrand political filmmaker, tho' there are numerous, self-conscious political statements throughout his work.

He's not known for delivering complex narrative structures, but his films are, like many movies, actually more complex narratively than they first appear. This applies to so many movies: film critics routinely call a plot 'simple', when it clearly isn't. Parts of a plot may seem simple (revolving around single words like 'revenge' or 'romance'), but how the plots are portrayed is seldom simple (even in Hong Kong cinema, where the quality of the screenplays is derided in Western film criticism).

Many actors and crew are happy to work with Ching Siu-tung, partly because they know that their work will be seen potentially by millions of people. Which's what it's all about. They also know that Ching is one of the great talents in action cinema, and that working on a Ching movie raises their own profile. And Ching will make them look very cool.

Also, movies directed by Ching Siu-tung will get released, a lot of people will see them, they won't be re-cut by studios or backers (or censored – usually), and there's a good chance that the marketing and promotion will be effective, and that they will be reviewed, and that they will have an after-life on TV, cable, DVD, etc. (All actors, East, or West, have been in or know about projects that were sat on for years, or never got released, or were distributed poorly, or were hacked about by distributors or studios.)

ASPECTS OF CHINESE ACTION MOVIES.

The following items are some of the aspects of Chinese and Hong Kong action movies, compared to Western (North American and European) action cinema:

• Acrobatic and athletic: one of the most obvious differences between Chinese and Western action cinema is the emphasis on acrobatic movement, on portraying the body in movement in space, on action like dance choreography and ballet, and action like circus performers, trapeze artists, jugglers, and street entertainers. (In Western choreography, acrobatics is part of the 'flash').

• Naturalism/ realism vs. fantasy: even the most 'realistic' of Chinese action movies contains more fantasy than most Western fantasy movies! Chinese action filmmakers never feel constrained to stick to notions such as 'realism' or 'naturalism'. A Chinese action scene can fly off in all sorts of directions.

• Humour: even in the grisliest and nastiest and most violent scenes in a Chinese action movie there might be humour. This is one aspect of Asian cinema that really jars with Western audiences, who like their serious moments to stay serious. Asian filmmakers (and Japanese animators in particular) are happy to mix in humour with drama, to pop melodramatic bubbles with laughs.

• Editing: Chinese action movies tend to be cut faster than Western action movies; but they don't resort to four angles of the same action (an irritating recent trend in Western cinema and TV).[6]

• Pacing: Chinese action movies are *much* faster, in terms of storytelling and pacing, than Western action movies. Yet there are many scenes where moments are expanded way beyond the requirements of the drama (emotional moments, for example, or, most famously, big action scenes which go far beyond the dramatic requirements of the scene).

• Cutting: the cuts occur in a different place in a Chinese action movie compared to its Western counterparts, and there is a different emphasis of the flow of movement, rhythm and of timing.

• The camera is very wild in Chinese action cinema: it doesn't stay on the horizontal, it is often tilted, it is often continually moving, and it is often at a low angle.

• The freedom of the camera: Chinese action filmmakers emphasize a feeling of total freedom to put the camera *anywhere* on the set.

• Framing: Chinese action movies tend to compose each shot for a specific movement.

• Shots: Chinese action cinema tends to construct its action scenes using short, individual shots, each one tied to a specific beat or movement or gesture, rather than master shots. In the West, master shot filmmaking is a standard approach, with the crew then moving in for close-ups, medium shots and inserts.

• The Chinese action team will film each individual moment, then turn around the camera and the lights to shoot the reverse angles, then go

---
[6] One reason is they haven't got *time* to film four shots of someone raising a glass to their mouth to drink.

back again to continue with the first side.

• Whole body shots: Chinese action movies typically include all of the body in their action scenes, rather than chopping it up into bits (a frustrating tendency in Western action cinema).

• Some shots are set up to be wildly over-the-top.

• Slow motion is everywhere (and at times filmmakers have had to slow down the martial arts performers because they are too fast for the camera to record their movements).

• Movement and reaction: Chinese action cinema is absolutely brilliant at evoking the impact of hits, the reactions of bodies in movement, the thud of a stunt guy on the ground. In Chinese action cinema, you see people *really* slamming into each other or the wall or the floor. There is always time taken for the reactions and the consequences of a particular movement or gesture.

• Visual effects: most Chinese action movies are filmed live, on the set, without resorting to post-production techniques. By contrast, since the 1990s, Western movies often include a lot of post-production technology. Budgetary reasons are key here, because Chinese action movies have a far lower budget than North American action movies (and visual effects are *very* expensive).

• In front of the camera: Chinese action movies recreate everything in front of the camera, and emphasize atmospheric elements, such as wind machines, smoke machines, fire, explosions, candles, and a host of wire effects and practical effects.

• Wirework: Chinese action filmmakers are without question the masters of using cables and movement of any cinema anywhere.

• Movement is much bigger and freer in Chinese action cinema compared to Western action cinema: bodies float, spin, leap and contort to an extraordinary degree in Chinese action cinema.

• Props: no filmmaking centre uses props as imaginatively as Hong Kong film crews (with a star like Jackie Chan, one of the all-time masters at deploying props in a fight scene).

• Weapons: in a Chinese action movie, anything in the immediate surroundings can be used as a weapon (including clothes and props like hats and umbrellas).

• Sound: Chinese movies tend to be filmed without live sound. The sounds that are added later mix punches and whooshes very high, but only use a few channels of sound; the movies also deploy sound effects in a different, highly stylized and definitely non-realistic manner. Western action movies, if they have the time and budget, often cram action scenes with large quantities of sounds, which tend to promote 'realism'/ 'naturalism' (sound fx fight with the music).

• Budgets: Hong Kong movies in the 1980s typically had budgets between US $100,000 and US $1,000,000.[7] The New Wave cinema of the early 1990s helped lead to rising costs, sometimes up to US $4 million (which was regarded as big budget), tho' around US $1.2 million was

---

[7] The budget for *The Big Boss*, a 1971 Bruce Lee picture, was $50,000.

typical (as was $650,000 – which was the budget of *A Chinese Ghost Story*). Needless to say, these are *very* low budgets compared to Western and Northern American budgets (similar American movies would cost 20 or 30 times more. When you see what Hong Kong filmmakers can do with 1.2 million US dollars, it is simply astounding).

SCRIPTS.

Almost all Hong Kong movies employ conventional narrative structures, including those of Ching Siu-tung. Altho' a common view among Western critics is that Hong Kong movies ignore conventional script structures, and focus on, say, action at the expense of narrative form, in fact they adhere to conventional structures. First acts climax just where you'd expect, for instance, and the finales begin right on cue.

Instead of applying the three-act model to all movies, a better way of thinking of acts in film scripts is to see them as 25-30 minutes narrative units (following Kristin Thompson in her book *Storytelling In the New Hollywood*). Thus, a two-hour movie will have *four*, not *three* acts (otherwise, you'd have a middle act lasting an hour). However, in Hong Kong, the industry usually releases films of 85-90 minutes, so that, yes, they are *three-act movies*. (And thus, for the action movies of Hong Kong, the *second act* is the big challenge – because any decent action movie can deliver a couple of great action scenes in the first act, and a Big Finale for the third act. But coming up with something in the middle which keeps the movie (and the audience) afloat is trickier).

One of the pluses of Chinese action cinema is that it tends to come in at 80 or 90 minutes. Whereas Western action movies of recent times tend to add an extra half-act or another whole act (i.e., 15 minutes or 25-30 minutes) to a movie, so they feel bloated and over-blown, Chinese action movies wind up the story in an hour-twenty or an hour-thirty. Because we've got people to meet afterwards, right? And dinner dates! And more movies to see! And *things to do*. Life in Hong Kong, for many citizens, is fast-paced, so a 2h 20m movie is simply *too long*.

Thus, Hong Kong and Chinese action movies are based on a three-act model – with each act running the customary 25-30 minutes. Altho' some critics complain that Hong Kong/ Chinese movies (in any genre) don't have decent scripts or stories, they do. In fact, they conform very much to traditional narrative structures. The first act, for example, is as conventional as in cinema from anywhere else.

MORE ON THE NARRATIVE STRUCTURE OF HONG KONG MOVIES.

Hong Kong movies are generally three-act movies running 80-90 minutes. The first act is typically the regular length (25-30 minutes), but the second act in an action movie is often shorter (20-25 minutes, rather than 25-30 minutes). This is partly because the second act usually explores characterization, back-stories and subplots, which can take a movie too far from action (it's also because the second act is by far the most challenging to write). Thus, the third and final act in an action movie might run for 35-40 minutes – partly because action movies are all about action and climaxes.

An action movie will typically have three big action set-pieces and three additional, smaller set-pieces – this applies to Hollywood action movies as well as Hong Kong action movies:

Act 1 climax
Act 2 climax
Act 3 climax
In addition, there will be further action sequences:
• The opening scene.
• Halfway thru act one.
• Halfway thru act two.

The finale of act three is often a reprise of the first act finale (on a bigger scale, with more at stake). The act two action set-piece might push the heroes back, have the villains triumphant for a moment, with all being staked in the final showdown. (They might steal the MacGuffin, or kidnap one of the heroes).

Action movies which open with an action set-piece sometimes use it to introduce the characters, and sometimes it will be a stand-alone sequence. After it, the exposition is delivered, as well as the narrative set-up or quest. This will be played out in the act 1 climax.

The action sequence halfway thru act one is often a reversal of fortunes for the heroes (it might split them up or injure one of them). If the movie didn't start with action, this is usually the first big action scene.

The action sequence halfway thru act two is often a chase or a raid or a heist – something to bring the heroes and the villains together. But nobody is a clear winner, and no one is sacrificed (sometimes more action scenes are added to act two).

POLITICS.

The social-political backgrounds of many Hong Kong historical pictures (including those of Tony Ching) can be reduced to simple components, like:

Hong Kong	versus	Mainland China
Capitalism		Communism
Westernization		Eastern values
The new		The old
Modernity		Tradition

And a good deal of the political and ideological content of historical Chinese movies boils down to simple dramatic oppositions:

West = technology (bad) ••• East = tradition (good)
West = guns (bad) ••• East = martial arts (good)

West = modern medicine (bad) ••• East = Chinese medicine (good)
West = exploitation (bad) ••• East = mercantile capitalism (good)
West = individualism (bad) ••• East = communities (good)

Thus, in film criticism of Hong Kong and Chinese cinema, the same simple oppositions are often employed:

Hong Kong	People's Republic of China
Hong Kong	Beijing
Hong Kong	North America
Hong Kong	Britain
Capitalism	Communism
Right-wing	Left-wing
Chinese culture	Western culture
Home	Exile
China	Chinatowns around the world
Chinese	Foreigners

So it's not only the *movies* that offer 'simplified' versions of politics, the *critics* do too.

CHING AND CHINA.

As an action director, Ching Siu-tung has overseen the action on many Western and non-Chinese productions; but his movies as director have tended to gravitate towards Chinese or Asian subject matter. Most of Ching's movies as director have been set in China, or are about Chinese characters. (And when he's directing a North American production, such as *Belly of the Beast*, the story is brought to Asia). As with the films of Tsui Hark, there is a celebration of Chinese tradition and culture in Ching's movies as director.

Stephen Teo, one of the better critics on Chinese cinema, pointed out that Tsui Hark's movies employ some of the icons and clichés of Chinese culture (such as acupuncture, martial arts, Peking Opera), in order to help make the movies appealing to outsiders. Yes – but as Tsui himself has noted, in the New Wave of Hong Kong cinema, the filmmakers were producing movies for the *local market*, and *not* for the global market (that came later).

This also applies to Ching Siu-tung's films, which celebrate traditional Chinese culture and practices. It's true that you could see that as a way of presenting the clichés and icons of China back to the home audience (just as every American cowboy flick contains numerous iconic elements which sell the Western/ frontier lifestyle back to the American audience).

Stephen Teo also talks of 'cultural nationalism', more an emotional desire among Chinese people living abroad for Chinese culture. Chinese nationalism, Teo asserts, is found everywhere in Chinese cinema, from *kung fu* flicks to New Wave films, from Mandarin historical epics to Cantonese melodramas (1997, 110-1). In the *kung fu* movies of the 1970s,

Teo identified an abstract nationalism in which *kung fu* heroes were using traditions (often from Shaolin) to fight foreign Manchus to restore the Chinese race (1997, 113).

Ching Siu-tung doesn't go as far as Tsui Hark in celebrating Chinese culture and society (that is one of Tsui's passions), but Tsui has certainly been a huge influence on Ching's form of cinema, and the cinematic nationalism in Tsui's work has definitely inspired Ching, too.

WUXIA PIAN.

Some eleven of Tony Ching's 22 films as director (from 1983-2019) can be classed as swordplay movies or *wuxia pian* (and also a good proportion of his films as action director). Thus, Ching can be regarded as one of the great experts of recent times in depicting swordplay on screen.

Wuxia[8] means swordsman/ martial fighter/ knight-errant (*wu* = military or armed; *xia* = hero, chivalrous. Known as *Mo hap* in Canontese. *Pian* = movies).[9] Thus, *wuxia pian* were swordplay pictures, and they tended to be filmed in Mandarin (shifts in the popularity of Mandarin versus Cantonese have occurred in the industry over the years).[10] *Kung fu* films referred to fist fighting, and were usually made in Cantonese (with the *Wong Fei-hung* movies as the typical local product). There's a North (Mandarin) vs. South (Cantonese) divide, too.

Wuxia movies were regarded as more historical and 'authentic' than *kung fu* movies; their trademarks included fantasy, the supernatural, performers flying,[11] 'Palm Power' (lightning bolts from the hands in the Taoist tradition), and visual effects. David Desser defined swordplay movies as 'period films, historical epics, mythological tales of magic, or action-spectaculars with colorful costumes' (2002, 31). *Kung fu* movies (from Canton) tended to be more 'realistic', emphasizing training and the body.

Jiangzhu means 'rivers and lakes': the term goes back at least to the 12th century and *The Water Margin* novel. *Jiangzhu* refers to the 'martial world' (and *wulin* to the 'martial forest'), in which the code of honour, of chivalry, of brotherhood, prevails. It's the code of living honourably that's invoked in the *jiangzhu*.

The *jiangzhu* and the *wulin*, the wandering world of a China that never really existed, is a mythical realm that Tony Ching has explored many times.

MORE ON WUXIA PIAN.

The genres of Chinese movies in the 1920s were largely defined by the Shaw Brothers (then known as Tianyi Film Company). Shaws was

---

8 *Wuxia*, according to director Chang Cheh, comes from *wu* = martial arts, and *xia* = chivalry.
9 Some titles of Hong Kong and Chinese movies are vague and generic – you'll see these words crop up time and again: *legend, story, hero, cop, dragon, weapon, dagger, sword, swordsman, warrior, butterfly, gambler*, etc.
10 Martial arts movies shifted in the early 1970s to Mandarin cinema, as Cantonese dwindled to nearly nothing in 1971-72. Martial arts movies, in Mandarin, dominated the box office. (Cantonese cinema declined in the middle to late 1960s, down to nearly nothing by 1972: 35 Cantonese films in 1970... in 1971, only one film... and in 1972, not a single one).
11 The powers of the floating warriors in *wuxia* films come from their martial arts skills, their *chi* – but they're not supernatural or superhuman powers.

founded in 1925 by Runjie Shaw. The popular genres of the time were *wuxia pian* (swordplay epics), *guzhuang pian* (classical, Chinese costume dramas), and *baishi pian* (historical movies).

Wuxia pian rapidly became popular in the 1920s: 250+ films were produced between 1928 and 1930. One of the most famous was *The Burning of Red Lotus Temple*[12] (Zhang Shichuan, 1928), regarded as the first martial arts masterpiece, which led to 18 sequels in 3 years. In the 1950s, Shaws was making fifty+ swordplay pictures a year. That meant they were releasing a film a week – incredible productivity – and most were in the martial arts genre.

Wuxia pian are typically set in ancient times, often in dynasties and courts, with chivalrous knights. The swordplay genre was associated with the Mainland, with Shanghai, while *kung fu* was a Southern, Hong Kong form. The *kung fu* genre is more 'realistic', often set in the Qing Dynasty, with foreigners as the villains. The heroes of Southern, *kung fu* movies include Wong Fei-hung and Fong Sai-yuk. When a swordsman is about to perform one of their special techniques, they often announce it: 'Flying Sword!'

COSTUMES.

The films of Ching Siu-tung are costume dramas even when they're set in the present day. Chinese, historical movies, historical martial arts movies and *wuxia pian* foreground *clothes* and *costumes*. Outlandish costumes are pretty much mandatory in a Chinese, historical movie, and of course this is also a big part of the Peking Opera tradition. Bright colours, tons of red and gold, rich blues and the brilliant yellows of Buddhism, are everywhere in Chinese, historical movies. And when it comes to depicting royalty or wealth, out come the luxurious frocks, the braid and embroidery, with an obsessive attention to detail (and as many action movies focus on guys, the costume, hair and make-up people seize upon the one or two female actresses with enthusiasm, lavishing attention on them). Purely as displays of costume design, Chinese, historical movies (and many action flicks), are sumptuous. And the films of Ching are some of the finest – one of his hallmarks is a feeling for flowing clothing flapping in the breeze as a swordsman (or swordswoman) makes yet another flying leap.

The wardrobe is also a significant ingredient in the action in a Chinese, historical movie: sometimes characters use clothing to attack opponents (Wong Fei-hung rushing thru a street brawl, for instance, using his jacket to whack people, in *Once Upon a Time In China 3*). In flying scenes, clothes're whipped by high wind, with the sound of flapping, twisting clothing mixed high (the sound of the wind is one of the fundamental sounds of the mysterious and the supernatural – not only in cinema, but anywhere). The shapes that the clothing makes are beautiful (especially in slow motion). The layers of loose, richly-hued clothing recalls the costumes that the Virgin Mary wears in Renaissance paintings in the

---

[12] It was adapted from the martial arts novel *Legend of Strange Heroes*.

West: painters in Europe in the 1400s-1600s had to learn how to depict robes and cloaks with deep, shadowy folds; it was part of the mythology of Christian art. And angels in Renaissance art also had billowing robes, emphasizing their spiritual energy as they descend from the heavens down to Earth).

Clothes are part of the stances and motion of martial arts, of course: flying scenes feature clothes flapping and billowing; in fights on the ground, clothes are grabbed, or they twist around bodies, or're used as weapons; when Jet Li's Wong Fei-hung prepares to battle, he flicks his outer garments back around his right leg, to leave room for movement.

And along with costumes, the hair and make-up in Chinese, historical movies is technically dazzling, but often also extravagant. There's no holding back in some of the fantastical, historical movies, which take place in the *jiangzhu*, the mythical China of yore. Then beards become so long you can trip over them, and wigs become so hairy they become a character in themselves (in fantasy flicks like *The Bride With White Hair* series, hair is a series of weapons in itself).

TEXTURES.

It's common in Hong Kong cinema to add textures in front of the camera, using practical effects: smoke is everywhere, for instance. Smoke in Hong Kong cinema is not a pretty effect that drifts in the background of a scene to enhance the lighting – it is used as a setting in itself, a real, physical presence in the scenes. Sometimes smoke provides the whole environment of a scene (and, yes, sometimes that billowing smoke is used to hide things). Items such as dust, earth, and leaves are thrown in front of the camera just before a take (sometimes petals, feathers, and dripping water). On a Tony Ching set, electric fans are always near the camera – clothes must flap and billow. And if it's a calm night, those fans will add the essential movement. (All sorts of fans – handheld, desk fans, larger fans, fans blowing down tubes to get the air close to the actors, etc.)

Hong Kong cinema developed the Akira Kurosawa School of Filmmaking – plenty of natural, elemental material on screen – rain, fire, smoke, wind, leaves, torchlight, candlelight, and more fire and more rain. Creating those textures also means filming outdoors in sometimes tough conditions (plus many night shoots). It means leading the production team up mountains and across rivers. And for the actors it means quite a bit of hardship (luxurious trailers are *not* usually part of a Hong Kong film production!).

To achieve those Kurosawan effects requires stamina, determination, and, perhaps above all, patience[13] (plus the resources of a fully-equipped studio with its technical staff). This is perfectionist filmmaking, getting every detail right, composing scenes and frames teeming with incident and gesture.

---

[13] Patience may be the number one requirement for a film director – the dogged determination to wait until you get what you're after.

AVAILABILITY

A *major* problem with approaching the cinema of any Hong Kong or Chinese film director is availability. You will stumble into the issue of availability as soon as you try to see anything other than the movies released in the Western world. Most of the films (and TV work) directed or action directed by Ching Siu-tung were produced for a Chinese market: the markets of Hong Kong and Mainland China are absolutely crucial.[14] This doesn't mean, tho', that the movies travel outside of China, either in their original form or in dubbed versions.

The language issue – Cantonese, Mandarin, English, whatever – is a minor one compared to general availability (subtitling is yet another issue). It's true that some of the key works directed by Ching Siu-tung are easy to obtain in the West – the *Swordsman* series, for instance, or *An Empress and the Warriors*.

But many movies are not easily available in the West, such as: *The Witch From Nepal, The Terracotta Warrior, The Longest Day, Conman In Tokyo* and *Belly of the Beast*. And gems of China cinema that Ching action-directed, like *Peking Opera Blues*, should be available in supermarket racks like Disney cartoons.

Even some of movies featuring big stars such as the two Chows – Chow Yun-fat and Stephen Chow (Chow Sing-chi) are not easily obtainable in the Western world. You should be able to find *Royal Tramp* or *Fight Back To School* anywhere.

That means that plenty of Tony Ching's films as an action director of the 1970s are not widely available, nor his films as an actor. Consequently, some movies directed by Ching Siu-tung, have not been explored fully in this study, including many released before 1980.

The issue of availability affects many celebrated filmmakers – you simply can't find many of their key works. The issue of quality is another consideration: many movies are only available in substandard prints, with bad soundtracks, or in butchered versions (some Hong Kong movies look like they were copied from beat-up release prints that have been kicking around Central for years, then re-dubbed onto video and back again). Despite new distribution systems like the internet, or streaming, or DVD and Blu-ray (or older ones like video, or broadcasting on television), it's amazing how many jewels of cinematic art remain in limbo, or are lost, or can only be bought in poor versions from dodgy, one-eyed former Buddhist monks in the scuzzy end of town (for extortionate prices).

Another issue is that the international and Western versions of Hong Kong and Chinese movies sometimes change the following: the music; the dialogue; the scripts (scripts are rewritten during dubbing); add new sound mixes; and whole scenes are dropped.

Thus often the Western/ international cuts of Asian movies are *not* in the form the filmmakers preferred. Tsui Hark, for instance, has complained many times that distributors have altered his movies for releases

---

[14] Hence, Hong Kong films are usually released with a Cantonese and a Mandarin soundtrack, which's the norm in Chinese cinema.

overseas.

The practice of dubbing the sound on afterwards in Chinese movies also extends to the stars: it was many years before Chinese movie audiences heard the real voices of Jackie Chan and Jet Li, for instance. Another consequence of dubbing is that the same group of actors tend to be heard in every movie. For international releases, scenes are often added, or cut, and music is altered, as is dialogue.

For research online, the Hong Kong Movie Database and Hong Kong Cinemagic are excellent (they have photos of the cast and crew, for instance – very helpful when Chinese movies are filled with unusual names (and many alternative names and spellings) in both Mandarin and Cantonese). Love Hong Kong Film has useful reviews.

Some of Tony Ching's movies as director

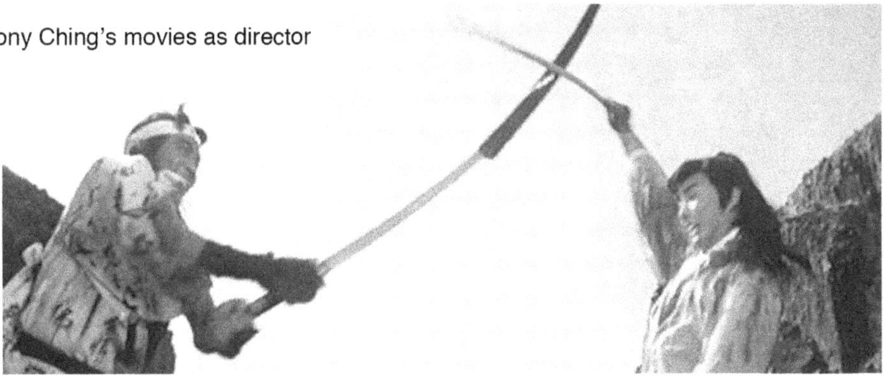

Duel To the Death (1983).

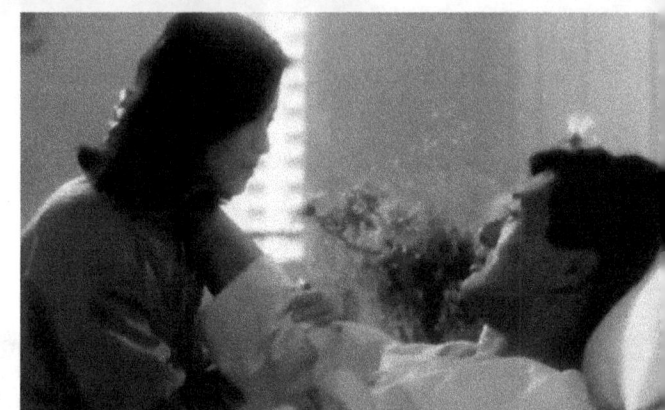

The Witch From Nepal (1986).

The Terracotta Warrior (1989).

The Swordsman 2 (1992).

The Heroic Trio (1993).

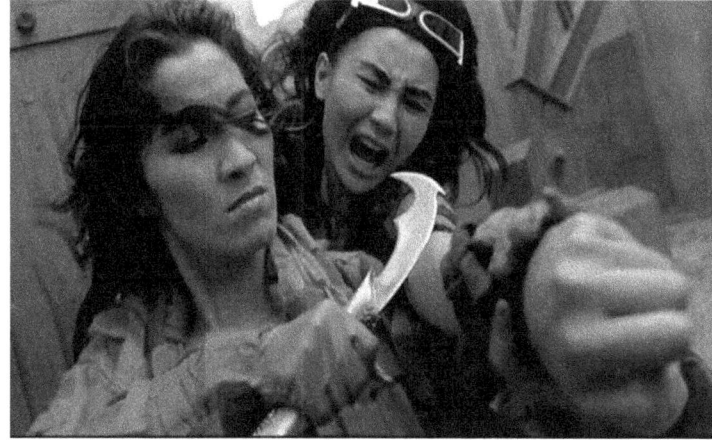

Dr Wai (1996).

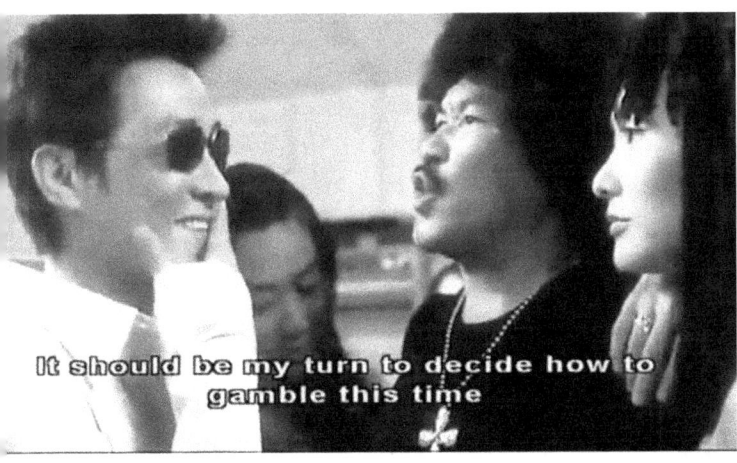

Conman In Tokyo (2000).

Naked Weapon (2002).

Belly of the Beast (2003)

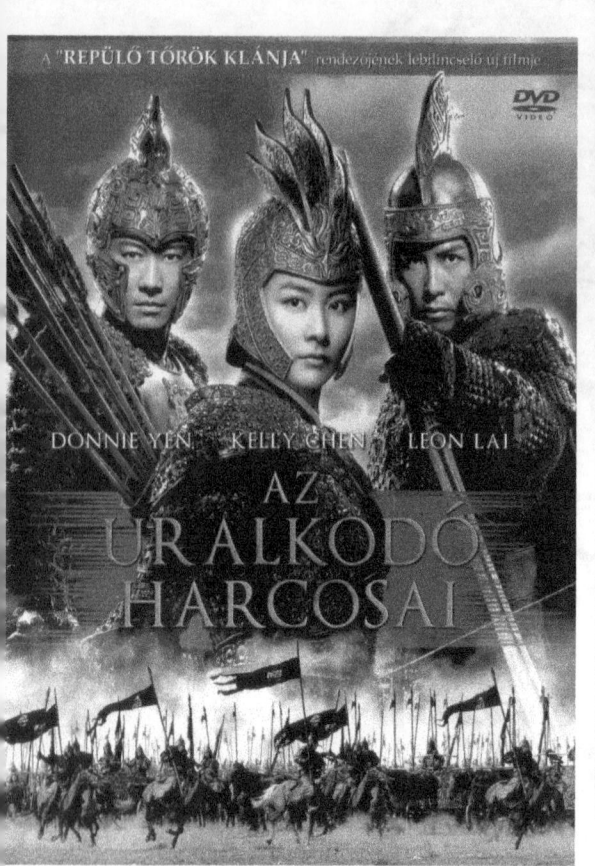 

An Empress and the Warriors (2008).

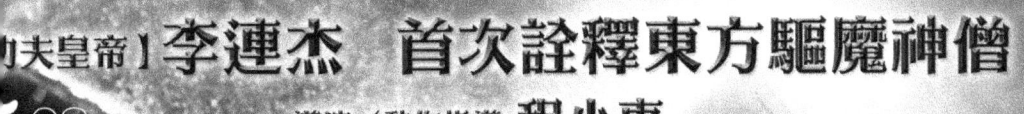

The Sorcerer and the White Snake (2011).

Jade Dynasty (2019).

3

TSUI HARK: BIOGRAPHY

INTRODUCTION

Tsui Hark is the dragon master of Chinese cinema (Stephen Teo calls Tsui a 'lion dancer among film directors' [173]). Yes – a master, a lion dancer, a *sifu*, a wizard, a dragon.

Tsui Hark is a one-man film industry – as a glance as his list of credits will show, along with setting up his own film company in 1983, Film Workshop.

Tsui Hark directs movies like a force of nature. The *energy* coming off the screen is stupendous! He is a fearless filmmaker, willing to try *anything* to get a good shot. And I do mean *anything*! That feeling of fearlessness, and wildness, coupled with imagination and technical brilliance, makes Tsui an incredibly *formidable* filmmaker. There are very few filmmakers on the scene today with those qualities in such abundance.

When you come back to a Tsui Hark picture after looking at other movies for a while, you realize, wow, this guy is *so* passionate about cinema, *so* willing to try anything, to experiment, to push the boundaries of what cinema can do, of what cinema can *be*. I've never felt, for example, that Tsui is a 'director for hire', unengaged with the material, or that he is merely punching through the shots as if he's on a factory floor.

No, this man is *on fire*.

BIOGRAPHY

Tsui Hark was born on January 2, 1951 (or February 15; some sources say 1950), in French Cochin China (Saigon, Vietnam). His name was originally Tsui Man-kong (he has also been known as Mark Yu). In Cantonese, his name is Chui Hak; in Mandarin, it's Xu Ke (Xu2 Ke4). He had sixteen siblings (from three marriages). His father was a pharmacist. Tsui changed his name from 'Tsui Man-kong' to 'Tsui Hark' because he thought it was too soft, and for his 'King Kong' nickname (1997, 136). It's ponounced 'Choy Hawk'. Tsui grew up in Saigon until the family moved to Hong Kong in 1966 (Tsui said he migrated around the age of 13, which makes it 1964; Lisa Morton says he was 14).[1]

Tsui Hark is a truly international filmmaker, as well as being a thoroughly Chinese/ Vietnamese one. After going to Hong Kong, he studied filmmaking in the U.S.A., at Southern Methodist University, Dallas in 1969 (for a year) before transferring to the University of Texas in Austin (Austin is a minor filmmaking centre in North America, with its own film culture, where filmmakers such as Richard Linklater are based). He also travelled around the U.S.A.

Tsui Hark graduated in 1975 (he studied for 2 years in Austin, where he was known as 'King Kong'). Tsui later worked in New York City: his first jobs were in television, not cinema: he gravitated from TV to film, as so many filmmakers have done (and as his fellow Hong Kong New Wave filmmakers did). His first jobs in Gotham were as a reporter for a Chinese TV cable station; he was a Chinese newspaper editor; worked with a community theatre group (New Art Drama Group); and helped to make a documentary about Chinatown (as a DP) called *From Spikes To Spindles* (Christine Choy, 1976). Tsui moved back to Hong Kong in 1976 (when he was 25).

Tsui Hark's film career got off to a roaring start with three outstanding pictures. Tsui's first theatrical movie as a director was *The Butterfly Murders* (1979), which combined martial arts, horror, sci-fi, comedy and romance. This was followed swiftly by *We're Going To Eat You* (1980) and *Dangerous Encounter of the 1st Kind* (1980) – both released in 1980.[2]

Directors often work in contrasts – if they've just done a comedy, they might fancy a drama next. Tsui Hark wanted to do something silly after his first three movies, which were 'very serious and very depressing' (LM, 47). Hence *All the Wrong Clues,* which was his first commercial hit (in 1981). And since then, Tsui had rarely let a year pass without releasing a movie as a director or producer (sometimes two! Sometimes three!). By 2014, Tsui had directed around 43 feature films.

As a producer, Tsui Hark has been responsible for masterpieces including: the *A Better Tomorrow* series, the *Chinese Ghost Story* series, the *Swordsman* series, *New Dragon Gate Inn* and *The Killer,* plus a host of

---

[1] Some accounts have Tsui coming to Hong Kong at the age of thirteen; others at fifteen (Tsui's year of birth is usually given as 1950 or 1951). It was in 1966 that Tsui's family moved to Canton.
[2] After *We're Going To Eat You*, Tsui Hark became 'very disappointed in myself', and considered giving up filmmaking.

hugely enjoyable films, such as: *Once Upon a Time in China 4, Once Upon a Time In China 6, Vampire Hunters, The Climbers* and *Black Mask*.

Tsui Hark is much more than a film director. Many directors do the job and go home afterwards. That's it. Some offer to produce other people's projects. Some form their own companies to develop and produce items they might direct themselves, or they might bring in colleagues they know. But only a few opt to take on numerous producing jobs, to the point where their career as a producer is as significant as their directing work. Tsui thus is not only a film director, *and* a film producer, he is also a movie mogul. (To do that amount of work, you have to *really* be committed).

In the press interviews for *Detective Dee and the Mystery of the Phantom Flame*, Tsui Hark was described by the cast and crew as brilliant, stern, tough, sweet, a free spirit, a teacher, boundlessly imaginative, and someone who lives in a different world from the rest of us.

Like many film directors, Tsui Hark has also filmed TV commercials (tho' not as many as some directors). They include *China Motion* (1998), for a telecommunications company on the Mainland (which was likened to the 1984 Apple ad); and *Singapore National Day* (1998).

Change and transformation are key elements in survival in the Hong Kong film industry, Tsui Hark asserted: if you don't change rapidly, you won't survive (LM, 22).

> For me, being commercial is very basic because you need the box office record in order to keep the investor surviving in this industry. But then, you need to be different. You need to be outstanding in terms of film. (2011)

Over the course of his film career, Tsui Hark has worked with practically every big star[3] in the Chinese film industry, as well as every action choreographer,[4] every DP and every major player in film production. (The Hong Kong film industry is small – everybody knows everybody else).

Tsui Hark's energy is legendary. Does he ever sleep? Can he survive on two or three hours sleep a night when he's shooting? (according to rumour). It does seem like that (it seems as if the last time that Tsui slept was in 1978). Tsui is one of those filmmakers who doesn't sit down on set, and is running at a high level of intensity as he's filming.

For instance, in more recent times, Tsui Hark has directed an enormous film production each year! *Detective Dee and the Mystery of the Phantom Flame* (2010), *The Flying Swords of Dragon Gate (*2011), *Young Detective Dee: Rise of the Sea Dragon* (2013) and *Taking Tiger Mountain*

---

[3] As a producer, Tsui Hark has been influential on the careers of Brigitte Lin, John Woo, Chow Yun-fat, Jet Li, Tony Ching Siu-tung, and many others. Jenny Kwok Wah-Lau noted that 'in Hong Kong, most people realize that it is Tsui Hark, the *producer* of *A Better Tomorrow,* who almost single-handedly revised and modernized the action genre and thus directly or indirectly launched the Hollywood careers of John Woo and superstars Chow Yun-Fat (through the same film) and Jet Li (through *Once Upon a Time In China*, which Tsui directed).' (in J. Geiger, 739).

[4] Tsui Hark has worked with practically every celebrated action choreographer in the Hong Kong film business: Sammo Hung, Jackie Chan, Yuen Bun, Yuen Woo-ping, Tony Ching Siu-tung, Yuen Wah, Lau Kar-leung, Xiong Xin-xin, etc.

(2014). Plus directing other movies, such as *Catching Monkey 3-D*.

There are times in the writing of this book (starting 2013-14), that I couldn't believe just how much Tsui Hark has achieved. Even compared to other workaholic film directors and producers, Tsui stands out. He really is a one-off. (Sometimes I wonder if 'Tsui Hark' is really a conglomerate of writers, producers, directors and visual effects mavens which uses the person we know and love, Tsui Hark, as their spokesman).

Tsui Hark's films have earned numerous awards. 1992 was one of Tsui's best years for awards – 21 nominations at the Hong Kong Film Awards – for *Once Upon a Time In China 2*, *New Dragon Gate Inn*, *The Swordsman 2* and *King of Chess*.

It's usually the same movies from Tsui Hark that feature in top ten lists – *Zu: Warriors From the Magic Mountain*, *Once Upon a Time In China*, *A Better Tomorrow*, *The Killer*, and occasionally the early, angry films: *We're Going To Eat You* and *Dangerous Encounters of the First Kind*. Tsui Hark has 7 films in the Top 100 Hong Kong Films in *Time Out*.

Some observers reckoned that Tsui Hark's film career stalled somewhat in the late 1990s and early 2000s, and that his movies didn't seem to find an audience during that time. Tsui said, yes, he had been trying different things; but he had also been doing the same thing he always did – make movies. It's all relative, tho', and box office success doesn't always match up with critical praise, or what a filmmaker regards as his best work. We all know filmmakers who produced much better movies than the ones that made the most $$$$$. However, commercial success *is* important if you want to produce movies on an ambitious scale (which Tsui often does).

A filmmaker of Tsui Hark's astounding abilities might be expected to go to Hollywood, as some of his Chinese contemporaries have done (notably John Woo, Tony Ching Siu-tung, Jet Li and Yuen Woo-ping). Tsui could've worked in Europe or Hollywood for all of his career following the big success of *Aces Go Places*. But Tsui's career in the U.S.A. has been patchy and somewhat disappointing. For example, instead of being hired by a film studio to helm a historical epic or a contemporary fantasy blockbuster (*Memoirs of a Geisha*, *X-Men*, *The Avengers* or *Pirates of the Caribbean*, say – Tsui would be perfect for *Pirates*!),[5] Tsui was hired to direct two Jean-Claude van Damme actioners. While John Woo directed *Mission: Impossible* and *Face-Off*, and Ringo Lam Ling-tung and Ronnie Yu made *Maximum Risk* and *Replicant* (Lam) and *51st State* and *Freddy vs. Jason* (Yu), high budget action movies, Tsui helmed a couple of van Damme movies which nobody has seen (altho' Woo also directed a Muscles From Brussels picture, *Hard Target*, 1993, as did Ringo Lam – *Maximum Risk*. Everyone in Hong Kong, it seemed, worked with van Damme at one time or another).[6]

Altho' the three Hollywood pictures helmed by Tsui Hark – *Knockoff*, *Double Team* and *Time and Tide* – were fascinating (and *Time and Tide* was

---

[5] And he delivered his own version in the *Detective Dee* series.
[6] The deal seemed to be: you can make an American production, but only if van Damme is the star.

as good an action thriller as has ever been made), the first two were still below the potential and talents of a director like Tsui. (All three were pointedly *not* filmed in the United States of America, however, but in Europa and Asia).

The anti-American politics in some of Tsui Hark's movies may have contributed towards his lack of success in the U.S.A (LM, 14), even tho' his movies are steeped in Hollywood/ Western cinema.

Following his uneven spree in Tinseltown, Tsui Hark has remained devoted to *Chinese* subjects – nearly *all* of his movies as director and producer have had Chinese settings, Chinese stories, Chinese themes and Chinese characters.

❀

Tsui Hark has gained a reputation for arguing with his collaborators, for taking over from other directors, or for directing when he should be producing. Or for being 'difficult'. Tsui doesn't understand it himself, but there are too many stories for there to be nothing in it! (Yet when actors meet him, expecting a difficult or irritable guy, they find someone very different).

When Tsui Hark is involved in a production, whether as producer, director, writer or backer, you know it's going to be interpreted as 'a Tsui Hark movie' (the same thing happens with filmmakers such as Steven Spielberg or George Lucas – they are such big, influential names in the movie business). Tsui is like that – he's the gorilla in the room that nobody talks about.

But one look at Tsui Hark's filmography, and you see an *enormous* amount of work, containing quite a few classics, plenty of ambitious works, and also several landmark movies in Chinese film history. Any history of recent cinema will have to include an entry on Tsui.

Tsui Hark is not a martial artist, and doesn't practise martial arts. He is not, as are Steven Spielberg, John Milius, Masamune Shirow and Mamoru Oshii, a gun nut.[7] For him, martial arts and guns are part of creating a fantasy.

Stephen Teo likens Tsui Hark's role in Hong Kong cinema to the Taoist priest in *A Chinese Ghost Story*: 'although he's not the hero, the Doaist plays the role of a *deus ex machina* in putting things right and making sure that the natural order is not disturbed' (1997, 228).

That Tsui Hark is a workaholic goes without saying. Tsui could've retired ages ago, or found a much easier way of making a buck than producing movies. Everybody who works with Tsui attests to his boundless energy. On the set, Tsui seems to wear everyone out with his relentless determination to get what he's after.[8] Tsui may come over in interviews as a slim and affable Asian guy who's happy to discuss any topic, but on the set[9] he must be a tough task-master at times.

[7] Tsui Hark doesn't know much about guns, or martial arts, and relies on other people for that. Instead, Tsui says that he's a fantasist, he imagines things that're the opposite of his real life.
[8] According to rumours, actors would bring their toothbrushes and pyjamas to the studio, because sometimes filming wended on for 48 or 72 hours.
[9] According to onlookers, the mood on a Tsui Hark set is pretty serious; not much goofing around, but getting on with the job.

When it comes to work, Tsui Hark's philosophy is simple: *if you see an opportunity, take it!* It sums up Tsui's incredible drive and ambition: this is a filmmaker with a truly extraordinary level of energy.

Hong Kong filmmakers are not known for their integrity: they have to survive, so, as Tsui Hark noted, 'they will do anything' (LM, 27). So it's the worst, because the filmmakers don't have integrity, but it's also the best because they are always looking for the next thing, for change.

Tsui Hark is happy to be interviewed and there are many interviews available of Tsui. Among the pieces on video and television about Tsui (apart from the usual 'making of' pieces on home releases), I would recommend *Action et Vérité* (2006), about the production of *The Blade*, a short but illuminating interview on *The Butterfly Murders*, *The Incredibly Strange Film Show* (1988-89), and *Yang ± Yin*, a documentary on gender in Chinese cinema directed by Stanley Kwan (1997).

Among Western movies, Tsui Hark has cited Orson Welles (*Citizen Kane*), Francis Coppola, John Ford, Roman Polanski (*Macbeth*), and Frederick Wiseman. The Marx Brothers have certainly influenced Tsui's comical style – not the speedy quips of Groucho, but the surreal bickering, and the silent comedy of Harpo.

You can see Tsui Hark's influence in many places: in movies like *The Stormriders* (Andrew Lau Wai-keung, 1999), *Initial D*, *He's a Woman, She's a Man*, *Ashes of Time*, and in filmmakers such as Wong Kar-wai, John Woo, Daniel Lee, Tony Ching, Peter Chan, Andrew Lau, Ang Lee, and Wong Jing. And the many Hong Kong movies which have emulated the Tsui Hark approach are easy to spot.

The *Once Upon a Time In China* series, as Jeff Yang put it, 'single-handedly revived the *kung fu* genre,[10] re-energized the Hong Kong film industry, and launched Mainland *wushu* master Jet Li's career into superstardom throughout Asia, and eventually, the world' (2003, 97). Tsui Hark called Jet Li a 'very special person'.

To make so many movies, as producer and director, means that Tsui Hark must *really* ♥ movies and filmmaking. Hooked on it, perhaps. Obsessive, even. Tsui is simply a natural filmmaker, like Jean-Luc Godard, Ingmar Bergman and Akira Kurosawa, filmmakers who seem to be live and breathe cinema. Tsui seems happiest when he's deep into production on a wild adventure in the archaic *jiangzhu*, or exploring a little-known corner of Chinese history.

Some have dubbed Tsui Hark the 'Asian Steven Spielberg', while others have noted that Spielberg should be so lucky.[11] Because Tsui goes beyond Spielberg in some respects. But they share numerous affinities: they are film buffs, they enshrine cinema of the past, they remake and update old classics,[12] they have taken on a wide variety of genres, they prefer storytelling with music and images above all, they are workaholics,

---

10 Certainly *Once Upon a Time In China* was a key movie in reviving the *kung fu* and martial arts genre – to the level of an artform.
11 Tsui has remarked: 'I don't know – it's unfair to him, I think. It's unfair to me too: he's so rich' (1997, 136).
12 Altho' Tsui Hark has gone back and remade the movies he enjoyed as a kid, he also knows that sometimes those movies one enshrined turn out to be silly and disappointing (LM, 23).

they work very fast on set, they make 'movie-movies', they are both moguls with their own companies, they have worked as film producers extensively, they adore visual effects and the artificiality of cinema, and they are master showmen.

Tsui Hark is also a movie and television generation filmmaker, like the 'movie brats' of the 'New Hollywood' era, such as Steven Spielberg, Brian de Palma, George Lucas and Jonathan Kaplan. There's no doubt that, like his N. American counterparts, Tsui is also remaking and updating many of the movies and TV shows he enjoyed as a youth. There is certainly a strong baby boomer aspect to Tsui's cinema, and a postmodern reworking of earlier forms and genres.

Stephen Teo calls Tsui Hark 'Hong Kong cinema's one genuine prodigy', a filmmaker who's 'primitive, even brutish', whose movies are too fast and too cluttered for some and remain indigestible. Teo reckons that the super-fast Tsui doesn't really have a counterpart in the West.

Stephen Teo:

Tsui Hark has what Hong Kong critics call a "devil's talent" (*gui cai*), a talent so broad and brilliant that it does not seem human. He is one of the prime movers in the industry and an original New Wave director who pushes his commercial instincts to the limit. (1998, 157)

Lisa Morton summed up Tsui Hark in her 2001 study:

Tsui Hark is unique in world cinema, a prolific filmmaker (Tsui has directed, written, produced and/ or acted in more than 60 feature films since 1979) who is also a master stylist; a political auteur and a populist; an artist with an obsessive private vision who is also commercially successful; and a filmmaker who seems to revel in deconstructing genres even while celebrating their tropes. (6)

Jeff Yang described Tsui Hark as 'one of the most reliable box office breadwinners of the eighties', a conceiver of new trends, a developer of new technologies and new cinematic techniques, a filmmaker who 'has generally beaten a path for the rest of the industry to follow' (2003, 95).

THE FILM CREDITS OF TSUI HARK

MOVIES AS DIRECTOR

The Butterfly Murders, 1979
We're Going To Eat You, 1980
Dangerous Encounters of the First Kind, 1980
All the Wrong Clues, 1981

Zu: Warriors From the Magic Mountain, 1983
Search For the Gods, 1983
Aces Go Places 3, 1984
Shanghai Blues, 1984
Working Class, 1985
Peking Opera Blues, 1986
Spirit Chaser Aisha, 1986
The Master, 1989
A Better Tomorrow 3, 1989
The Swordsman, 1990
Once Upon a Time in China, 1991
The Banquet, 1991
The Raid, 1991
Once Upon a Time in China 2, 1992
Twin Dragons, 1992
Once Upon a Time in China 3, 1993
Green Snake, 1993
Once Upon a Time in China 5, 1994
The Lovers, 1994
The Chinese Feast, 1995
Love In the Time of Twilight, 1995
The Blade, 1995
Tristar, 1996
Double Team, 1997
Knock Off, 1998
Time and Tide, 2000
The Legend of Zu, 2001
Black Mask 2: City of Masks, 2002
In the Blue, 2005
Seven Swords, 2005
Triangle, 2007
Missing, 2008
All About Women, 2008
Detective Dee and the Mystery of the Phantom Flame, 2010
The Flying Swords of Dragon Gate, 2011
Young Detective Dee: Rise of the Sea Dragon, 2013
Catching Monkey 3-D, 2013
The Taking of Tiger Mountain, 2014
Journey To the West: Conquering the Demons, 2017
Detective Dee and the Four Heavenly Kings, 2018
The Battle At Lake Changjin, 2021
The Battle At Lake Changjin: Water Gate Bridge, 2022

MOVIES AS PRODUCER

All the Wrong Spies, 1983
A Better Tomorrow, 1986
The Laser Man, 1986
A Chinese Ghost Story, 1987
A Better Tomorrow 2, 1987
The Big Heat, 1988
Gunmen, 1988
Diary of a Big Man, 1988
The King of Chess, 1988/ 1992
The Master, 1989
A Better Tomorrow 3, 1989
The Killer, 1989
Just Heroes, 1989
The Terracotta Warrior, 1989
The Swordsman, 1990
A Chinese Ghost Story 2, 1990
A Chinese Ghost Story 3, 1991
Once Upon a Time in China, 1991
New Dragon Gate Inn, 1992
The Swordsman 2, 1992
The Wicked City, 1992
Once Upon a Time in China 2, 1992
Once Upon a Time in China 3, 1993
Green Snake, 1993
The Swordsman 3: The East Is Red, 1993
Once Upon a Time in China 4, 1993
Once Upon a Time in China 5, 1994
The Lovers, 1994
Burning Paradise, 1994
The Chinese Feast, 1995
The Blade, 1995
Shanghai Grand, 1996
A Chinese Ghost Story: The Tsui Hark Animation, 1997
Once Upon a Time in China and America, 1997
Time and Tide, 2000
The Legend of Zu, 2001
Old Master Q, 2001
Tsui Hark's Vampire Hunters, 2002
Black Mask 2: City of Masks, 2002
Xanda, 2004
Seven Swords, 2005
The Warrior, 2006
Triangle, 2007
Missing, 2008
All About Women, 2008

Detective Dee and the Mystery of the Phantom Flame, 2010
The Flying Swords of Dragon Gate, 2011
Young Detective Dee: Rise of the Sea Dragon, 2013
Christmas Rose, 2013
The Taking of Tiger Mountain, 2014
Sword Master, 2016
The Thousand Faces of Dunjia, 2017
Journey To the West: Conquering the Demons, 2017
Detective Dee and the Four Heavenly Kings, 2018
The Climbers, 2019
The Battle At Lake Changjin, 2021
The Battle At Lake Changjin 2, 2022

By any standards, that list of film credits is completely remarkable! And it's a selective list, which doesn't include everything that Tsui has done.[13] You have to add writing credits to that list, and entries in anthology films, plus several TV series, as well as plenty of acting and cameos. And design work, editing and visual effects.

Up to 2013, Tsui Hark had writing credits on 36-42 movies,[14] story credits for 10 films, director credits for 43-45 movies, producer credits for 58-62 productions, and actor credits for 26 films.

Tsui Hark has writing credits on most of the movies he's directed, and he has producer credits on most of them, too. Which means that Tsui can properly be regarded as an *auteur*. The key production credit in many respects, in relation to the cinema of Tsui (and most cinema), is *producer*, more even than director or writer. (But Tsui is also more than a producer, director and writer, he is also a movie mogul with his own production company and visual effects company).

Among the movies directed by Tsui Hark, the following are masterpieces: *Once Upon a Time In China 1*, *Once Upon a Time In China 2*, *Once Upon a Time In China 3*, *Seven Swords*, *Detective Dee and the Mystery of the Phantom Flame*, *Young Detective Dee*, *Zu: Warriors From the Magic Mountain*, *The Flying Swords of Dragon Gate*, *The Taking of Tiger Mountain*, *Shanghai Blues*, *Peking Opera Blues* and *The Swordsman*. Many other movies directed by Tsui are fantastically enjoyable cinema: *Green Snake, The Blade, The Master, Detective Dee and the Four Heavenly Kings, The Legend of Zu* and *Time and Tide*. Only one or two movies with Tsui at the helm are disappointing: *Triangle* (co-directed with To and Lam), and *All About Women*.

One striking aspect of Tsui Hark's output is that fully half or more of his movies as director and producer have been historical pictures, a much greater ratio than most other filmmakers. Tsui is a specialist in costume films, and most of his masterpieces have also been historical movies. Notice, too, that in the more recent part of his career, the 2000s and

---

13 *The Legend of Famen Temple* (*Fa Men Si Mi Ma*), another historical fantasy, was rumoured in 2016-2017, based on a novel by Huang Shang Jin-yu, and starring Kenny Lin, Chen Kun, Zitao Huang and Xun Shou.
14 44 films to 2016, at Internet Movie Database.

2010s, Tsui has been focussing on history – going back to the mid-20th century in the war pictures (*Tiger Mountain, Lake Changjin*) or Ancient China (*Detective Dee*). The last feature films set in the contemporary era was in 2008 (*All About Women* and *Missing*).

The production roles are important, because we know that Tsui Hark is a very hands-on producer. The role of a producer varies widely, from someone way back in a project's history who oversaw one of the numerous script rewrites to a producer who oversees every aspect of the production.

Well, we know that Tsui Hark has performed second unit direction on some movies he's produced, and also co-directed some of them. And when Tsui insists that he *didn't* direct some of the movies (such as those directed by Tony Ching Siu-tung), his influence as writer or co-writer and of course as producer can felt everywhere in those movies.

TSUI HARK AS FILM PRODUCER

The movies that were produced by Tsui Hark can be regarded as part of his *œuvre* to a greater degree than many films which other directors have acted as a producer on – because Tsui is a hands-on producer.

But what is a film producer? Critics don't really know, yet the Western/ Hollywood film industry is a producer-led, producer-based business, and in the Hong Kong industry, too, producers lead the way. Among the many functions a good film producer does is: (1) buying and developing material; (2) hiring writers; (3) putting together deals; (4) approaching investors, and finding backing/ money/ resources; (5) hiring directors and other personnel; (6) over-seeing the all-important pre-production, which includes 100s of elements; (7) casting; (8) over-seeing shooting; (9) over-seeing post-production (again, this involves 100s of ingredients); (10) music, selecting composers; and (11) publicity, marketing, advertizing.

Tsui Hark has performed all of those tasks many times, and there's no doubt that as a film producer he is right in there, selecting and developing projects, and shepherding them to pre-production (that's when a movie is really made). If he's sometimes a dictator, well, he replies, the creative process needs that.[15]

Among Tsui Hark's numerous production credits, apart from acting as the producer on the movies he's directed, are (Tsui also has writing credits on most of these movies):

• *All the Wrong Spies* (Teddy Robin, 1983), a sequel to *All the Wrong Clues* (dir. by Tsui Hark). Written by Raymond Wong Pak-min, it starred George Lam, Teddy Robin, Paul Chun Pui, Brigitte Lin, Shing Fui-on, Joe Junior, Tsui Hark and Anders Nelsson. Tsui and his wife Nansun Shi Nan-sheng are credited as production designers.

---
15 Is he a dictator? Yes, he admits, 'But the creative process needs that'.

• The two *A Better Tomorrow* movies[16] (1986 and 1987).

• *The Laser Man* (1986), was executive produced by Tsui Hark and Sophie Lo, written, directed and co-produced by Peter Wang, and starred Marc Hiyashi, Peter Wang, Tony Leung and Sally Yeh.

• *Gunmen* (Kirk Wong, 1988),[17] starring Tony Leung, Adam Cheng, Elvis Tsui, Waise Lee and Carrie Ng.

• *The Big Heat* (Johnny To & Andrew Kam, 1988), written by Gordon Chan, starring Waise Lee, Philip Kwok, Paul Chu-kong, Stuart Ong Sai Kit, Michael Chow Man Kin, Ken Boyle and Joey Wong. Tsui Hark appears in some credits as the co-director in this very troubled production.

• *Diary of a Big Man* (1988) was produced by Tsui Hark, directed by Chor Yuen, and starred Chow Yun-fat, Joey Wong, Sally Yeh, Waise Lee and Kent Cheng.

• *A Chinese Ghost Story* (Tony Ching Siu-tung, 1987), starring Leslie Cheung, Joey Wong and Wu Ma.

• *A Chinese Ghost Story 2* (Tony Ching Siu-tung, 1990) starring Leslie Cheung, Joey Wong, Michelle Reiss, Jacky Cheung and Waise Lee.

• *A Chinese Ghost Story 3* (Tony Ching Siu-tung, 1991), starring Tony Leung Chiu-wai, Joey Wong, Jacky Cheung and Nina Le Chi.

• *I Love Maria* (a.k.a. *Roboforce*, 1988), was a Hong Kong version of *RoboCop* (1987), co-produced by Tsui Hark with John Sham, directed by David Chung Chi-man,[18] starring Sally Yeh, Tsui Hark, John Sham and Tony Leung.

• *The Killer* (John Woo, 1989), starring Chow Yun-fat, Danny Lee, Shing Fui-on and Sally Yeh.

• *Deception* (a.k.a. *Web of Deception*, David Chiang, 1989), starring Brigitte Lin, Joey Wong and Pauline Wong.

• *The Terracotta Warrior* (Tony Ching Siu-tung, 1989), starring Zhang Yimou, Gong Li and Yu Rongguang.

• *Just Heroes* (a.k.a. *Tragic Heroes*, 1989) was a benefit movie for the Hong Kong directors' union. It starred a host of names, including David Chiang, Danny Lee, Chen Kuan-tai, Stephen Chow, Lo Lieh, Ti Lung, Cally Kwong, Wu Ma, Shing Fui-on, James Wong Jim, Bill Tung, Zhao Lei and Tien Niu.

• *Spy Games* (David Wu Tai-wai, 1990) was a spy movie spoof directed by Wu, who's edited many of Tsui's movies. It was written by Ng Man-fai, Philip Cheng, Lam Kee-to and Lau Tai-mok, and starred Joey Wong, Kenny Bee, Noriko Izumoto, Waise Lee and Shut Yam.

• *The Raid* (Tony Ching Siu-tung and Tsui Hark, 1991) was a 1930s adventure comedy co-written by Tsui Hark and Yuen Kai-chi, and starring Jacky Cheung, Dean Shek, Tony Leung, Paul Chu, Fennie Yuen and Joyce Godenzi.

• *The Swordsman* (King Hu *et al*, 1990), starring Sam Hui, Cecilia Yip, Yuen Wah, Jacky Cheung and Cheung Man.

---

16 The *Better Tomorrow* movies inevitably inspired cash-ins – such as *Return To Better Tomorrow* (Wong Jing, 1994).
17 Critics have discerned the influence of Tsui Hark in *Gunmen* (which he produced), in the romantic atmosphere, and in the action.
18 Tony Ching Siu-tung was 2nd unit director.

- *The Swordsman 2* (Tony Ching Siu-tung, 1991), starring Jet Li, Brigitte Lin, Rosamund Kwan, Michelle Reiss and Fennie Yuen.
- *The Swordsman 3: The East Is Red* (Tony Ching Siu-tung & Raymond Lee, 1993), starring Brigitte Lin, Yu Rongguang, Joey Wong and Eddie Ko.
- *Dragon Inn* (a.k.a. *New Dragon Gate Inn*, Raymond Lee, 1992), starring Tony Leung, Brigitte Lin, Maggie Cheung and Donnie Yen.
- *The Wicked City* (*Yiu Sau Do Si*, dir. Peter Mak Tai-kit, 1992), a live-action version of the Japanese *animé* (1987), staring Leon Lai Ming, Jacky Cheung Hak-yow, Michelle Reiss and Tatsuya Nakadai.
- *Iron Monkey* (Yuen Woo-ping, 1993), co-written by Tsui Hark with Tang Pik-yin and Lau Tai-mok, and starring Donnie Yen, Yu Rongguang and Jean Wong.
- *The Magic Crane* (Benny Chan, 1993), co-written by Tsui Hark (with Jobic Chui Daat-Choh), and starring Anita Mui, Tony Leung Chiu-wai, Rosamund Kwan and Damian Lau.
- *Burning Paradise*, a.k.a. *Red Lotus Temple* (Ringo Lam Ling-tung, 1994), starring Willie Chi, Wong Kam-long and Carman Lee.
- *Once Upon a Time In China 4* (Yuen Bun, 1993), co-written by Tsui and Tang Pik-yin, was released only four months after the third *Once Upon a Time In China* movie, and starred Vincent Zhao, Jean Wong, Xiong Xin-xin, Max Mok and Lau Shun.
- *Shanghai Grand* (Poon Man-kit, 1996), was a period gangster tale co-written by Sandy Shaw, Matthew Chow Hoi-kwong and Poon Man-kit. It starred Andy Lau Tak-wah, Leslie Cheung and Lau Shun.
- *Black Mask* (Daniel Lee Yan-kong, 1996) was a wild superhero adventure co-written by Koan Hui-on, Teddy Chan Tak-sum and Joe Ma Wai-ho, and starring Jet Li, Karen Mok, Lau Ching-wan, Francoise Yip, Moses Chan and Anthony Wong.
- *Once Upon a Time in China and America* (Sammo Hung Kam-bo, 1997), was co-written by Roy Szeto Cheuk-hon, Shut Mei-yee, Sharon Hui Sa-long, Philip Kwok and So Man-Sing, and starred Jet Li, Rosamund Kwan, Xiong Xin-xin, Chan Kwok Pong, Richard Ng and Jeff Wolfe.
- *Old Master Q* (2001) was co-written by Tsui Hark with Roy Szeto Cheuk-hon, Herman Yau and Man Choi-lee, exec-prod. by Charles Heung and Tsui Hark, and dir. by Herman Yau.
- *Tsui Hark's Vampire Hunters* (2002) was produced and written by Tsui Hark, and dir. by Wellson Chin Sing-wai.
- *Xanda* (*Sanda*, 2004) was wr. by Kai-Cheung Chung, Derick Lau, Ask Lee, Xiao-Long Lin and Tsui Hark, exec-prod. by Satoru Iseki, Nansun Shi Nan-sheng and Le Qun Song, prod. by Tsui Hark, and directed by Marco Mak Chi-sin.
- *The Warrior* (literal title: *Wong Fei-hung: Brave Into the World,* 2006) was a Wong Fei-hung movie as an animation, directed by Tiger Fu Yin and Chen Yue-Hu and produced by Yang Yong.
- *Sword Master* (Derek Yee, 2016) was a 3-D *wuxia pian* produced by Tsui Hark and co-written by Tsui with Derek Yee and Chun Tin-nam.

Another aspect is immediately obvious: there were years when Tsui

Hark was directing not one but two movies! And in some years, even more! In 1995: *The Chinese Feast, Love in the Time of Twilight* and *The Blade*! (In the North American film industry, it's typical for a film director to direct every three years).

TSUI HARK AS WRITER

Among Tsui Hark's writing for cinema credits are: *Di yu wu men, Dangerous Encounters of the First Kind, All the Wrong Clues, A Better Tomorrow 2*,[19] *Tit gaap mou dik maa lei aa, The Master, A Better Tomorrow 3: Love and Death in Saigon, A Chinese Ghost Story, A Chinese Ghost Story 3, Once Upon a Time in China, The Banquet, Twin Dragons, The Swordsman, Once Upon a Time in China 2, New Dragon Gate Inn, Once Upon a Time in China 3, The Swordsman 3: The East Is Red, Once Upon a Time in China 4, Iron Monkey, Ching Se, Yiu sau dou si, The Magic Crane, Once Upon a Time in China 5, The Chinese Feast, Love In the Time of Twilight, The Lovers, The Blade, Da san yuan, Black Mask,* the animated *Chinese Ghost Story, Time and Tide, Old Master Q, The Legend of Zu, Black Mask 2: City of Masks, The Era of Vampires, Xanda, Seven Swords, Missing, All About Women, Flying Swords of Dragon Gate, Young Detective Dee: Rise of the Sea Dragon, Sword Master, Detective Dee and the Four Heavenly Kings, The Thousand Faces of Dunjia* and the two *Battle of Lake Changjin* movies.

Tsui Hark has also worked uncredited as a writer, sometimes helping out pictures that are in trouble. For ex, Tsui contributed (along with Gordon Chan) to *Dr Wai* (Tony Ching Siu-tung, 1996), a Jet Li actioner.

Lisa Morton noted that Tsui Hark has only made one proper sci-fi movie – *I Love Maria* (a.k.a. *Roboforce*). Actually, the two *Black Mask* movies are science fiction. But Tsui has acknowledged that he hasn't done much in sci-fi – he prefers Ancient Chinese fantasy and mythology.

However, Tsui Hark has certainly directed movies which portray savage realms that come across like post-apocalyptic worlds: the brutish martial arts world (*jiangzhu*) of *The Blade*[20] and *Seven Swords* come to mind.

---

19 *A Better Tomorrow 2* (1987) was written and directed by John Woo, produced by Tsui Hark, with action direction by Tony Ching Siu-tung, and starred Chow Yun-fat, Dean Shek, Ti Lung, Leslie Cheung and Emily Chu.
20 Paul Fonoroff reckoned that 'if movies were judged on visuals alone, *The Blade* would certainly rank as one of the decade's most stunning motion pictures' (527).

TSUI HARK AND TELEVISION

Tsui Hark first worked in television in the late 1970s; his first TV shows were *Golden Dagger Romance* (1978), made for C.T.V., adapted from a novel by Gu Long (during Tsui's 6 months there) and *Aries, Scorpio, Aquarius* (T.V.B., 1978). Tsui was also one of five directors (Ringo Lam Ling-tung was another) of *The Family* (1978, at T.V.B.), a 104-episode soap opera ('people die, get rich, get divorced', as Tsui summed it up [1997, 133]). Tsui came back to television several times – for the *Wong Fei-hung* and *Seven Swordsmen* TV series, for example.

> I went to film school simply because I like to express my feelings on certain issues through film, which was a pretty popular medium during the 1960s. We spent a lot of time in movie theaters. At that time I was already thinking how to make Chinese cinema more interesting.

For Stephen Teo, Tsui Hark's cinema is a vivid embodiment of the maturation of the New Wave, and the postmodernism of commercial cinema:

> Using Tsui as a yardstick, the postmodern phenomena grew from a ragbag of causes and effects: new wave æsthetics mixed with Cinema City-style slapstick, anxiety over 1997 and the China syndrome, the assertion of Hong Kong's own identity as different from China, and a new sexual awakening arising from an increasing awareness of women's human rights and the decriminalisation of homosexuality. (1997, 246)

CINEMA CITY

Tsui Hark was part of the group of filmmakers at Cinema City (from 1981). A new studio, Cinema City wasn't independent – it was owned by Golden Princess. It had been founded by Raymond Wong Pak-min, Karl Maka (b. 1944) and Dean Shek in 1979 (as the Fun Dao Film Company). The so-called 'Gang of Seven' at Cinema City were Tsui, Maka, Wong, Shek, Teddy Robin Kwan, Eric Tsang and Tsui's wife Nansun Shi Nan-sheng. As Tsui recalled, they would consider everything, go thru scripts at length and discuss them.

All the Wrong Clues… For the Right Solution (1981) was Tsui Hark's first Cinema City production: it was produced by Karl Maka and Dean Shek, written by Roy Szeto Cheuk-hon (a regular collaborator with Tsui) and Raymond Wong Pak-min, and starred George Lam, Teddy Robin Kwan, Maka and Wong Tso-sze (for some critics, this movie announced the end of the Hong Kong New Wave).

Aces Go Places 3 (a.k.a. Mad Mission 3, 1984) was another installment in the successful Aces Go Places franchise from Cinema City (the earlier films were released in 1982 and 1983. The movies were the top films of each year (the first Aces Go Places grossed HK $26 million[21] when ticket prices were HK $15 (= U.S. $1.95).) It was produced and written by Raymond Wong Pak-min, and starred Sam Hui, Karl Maka and Sylvia Chang. According to Stephen Teo, 'Tsui's own dynamic style of filmmaking initiated a level of structural experimentation which was to be highly influential' (153).

The 'Cinema City style' emphasized comedy above all, stunts, visual effects, big budgets, and movies constructed by a creative team. For a period in the 1980s, Cinema City cornered the market for theatrical comedies. About 17% of films were comedies between 1985 and 1997 in Hong Kong.

FILM WORKSHOP

In 1984 Tsui Hark founded Film Workshop with his wife, Nansun Shi Nan-sheng (he had decided to create a company during post-production of Zu: Warriors From the Magic Mountain; it was partly because Cinema City were only interested in making comedies). Film Workshop is based in Kowloon Bay.

Terence Chang[22] worked as general manager at Film Workshop in the 1980s (at Nansun Shi Nan-sheng's invitation). Following Tsui Hark's dispute with John Woo over The Killer and A Better Tomorrow 3,[23] Chang left with Woo. Chang described his time at Film Workshop thus:

> The first year was really exciting. The company was new, vibrant, and a lot of great films came from that time. Tsui Hark was very idealistic. He wanted to round up the best directors in Hong Kong and put them under one roof. He wanted to create an environment where all the directors, under his leadership, could be given the opportunity and nourishment to make artistic, yet commercial pictures.

The productions of Film Workshop include: Shanghai Blues (1984), The Master (1989), King of Chess (1992), The Swordsman 2 (1992), Wicked City (1992), New Dragon Gate Inn (1992), Once Upon a Time in China 2 (1992), The East Is Red (1993), The Magic Crane (1993), Iron Monkey (1993), Once Upon a Time in China 3 (1993), Once Upon a Time in

---

21 There are typically 7.75 Hong Kong dollars to the U.S.A. dollar. (So when a movie makes HK $30 million in theatrical release in Hong Kong, that equals US $3.87 million).
22 John Woo's regular producer, Terence Chang (b. 1949), had studied in New York and Oregon before working at Golden Harvest and in TV before joining Film Workshop. Chang also worked at D. & B.
23 He rushed his own sequel to A Better Tomorrow into theatres, for instance (which he had co-produced), to beat John Woo's sequel (altho' Woo doesn't like doing sequels).

China 4 (1993), *Green Snake* (1993), *A Chinese Ghost Story: The Tsui Hark Animation* (1997), *Knockoff* (1998), *Time and Tide* (2000), *The Era of Vampires* (2002), *Xanda* (2004), *Seven Swords* (2005), *Triangle* (2007), *All About Women* (2008) and the *Detective Dee* movies.

Tsui Hark has worked with Golden Harvest for much of his career; they have enjoyed many successes. However, they have also fallen out – over the release of *Zu: Warriors From the Magic Mountain*, for instance. And in the late 1990s, Golden Harvest sued Tsui for over-runs on 8 films (and Tsui's lawyers responded with a counter-suit for revenue from the *Once Upon a Time In China* pictures).

SOME GREAT MOMENTS IN TSUI HARK'S WORK

- Avoiding the cannibals in *We're Going To Eat You*
- The finale of *Zu*
- Meeting under the bridge in *Shanghai Blues*
- Backstage in *Peking Opera Blues*
- Chow Yun-fat versus the tank in *A Better Tomorrow 3*
- Maggie Cheung in *New Dragon Gate Inn*
- The first act of *Once Upon a Time In China*
- The ladders duel in *Once Upon a Time In China*
- Leslie Cheung in the haunted inn in *A Chinese Ghost Story*
- Wu Ma's Taoist dance in *A Chinese Ghost Story*
- Jet Li versus Donnie Yen in *Once Upon a Time In China 2*
- The Lion Dance competition in *Once Upon a Time In China 3*
- Jet Li in a clinch with Brigitte Lin in *The Swordsman 2*
- The watery finale of *Green Snake*
- The musical/ romantic montage in *The Lovers*
- The final duel in *The Blade*
- The motorcycle chase in *Black Mask*
- The market chase in *Knock-Off*
- The apartment fire-fight in *Time and Tide*
- The arrival of the warriors in *Seven Swords*
- Jet Li vs. Gordon Liu in *Flying Swords of Dragon Gate*
- Andy Lau and Jinger in *Detective Dee*
- The sea monster in *Young Detective Dee*
- The snow tiger scene in *The Taking of Tiger Mountain*
- The Battle of the Buddhas in *Journey To the West*
- The monster battle in *Detective Dee 3*

Tsui Hark on the sets of the Detective Dee films.

On the set of Flying Swords of Dragon Gate (above).

PART TWO

A CHINESE GHOST STORY

1

A CHINESE GHOST STORY

Sin Nui Yau Wan

INTRO TO *A CHINESE GHOST STORY*.
The *Chinese Ghost Story* movies are:

A Chinese Ghost Story (1987)
A Chinese Ghost Story 2 (1990)
A Chinese Ghost Story 3 (1991)
A Chinese Ghost Story: The Tsui Hark Animation (1997)

A Chinese Ghost Story was remade in 2011 (and dedicated to Leslie Cheung).

A Chinese Ghost Story (1987, Mandarin: *Qiannu Youhun* = *Sien: Female Ghost*, a.k.a. *Fair Maiden, Tender Spirit*), was one of those movies where everything works, and the mix of elements is just gorgeous. This is a golden, 100% killer of a movie.[1]

A Chinese Ghost Story has everything going for it: it is among the finest fantasy and action movies ever; it boasts a finale as grand as any in cinema; it tackles the most profound themes; it possesses a perfectly achieved tone and attitude; it features two incandescent stars; it is helmed by two of the greatest action directors in history; and it is brilliant filmmaking.

A Chinese Ghost Story was produced by Film Workshop/ Cinema City written by Yuen Kai-Chi, produced by Tsui Hark, Claudie Chung Jan and Qianqing Liu, exec. prod. by Zhong Zheng, and directed by Tony Ching Siu-tung. Music was by the great James Wong Jim,[2] Romeo Diaz, David Wu and Dai Lemin, editing by David Wu Tai-wai, production design by Hai Chung-Man, art dir. by Kenneth Yee Chung-man, costumes by Shirley Chan and Kitty Ho Wai-Ying, hair by Peng Yen-Lien, make-up by Renming Wen and Man Yun-Ling, visual fx by Ma Xian Liang, sound by Xiaolong

---
[1] For more on the *Chinese Ghost Story* films, see my companion book.
[2] This was the first James Wong Jim contribution to Tsui's movies (along with *Shanghai Blues*).

Cheng, David Wu and Qun Xue, with photography by Poon Hang-Sang, Sander Lee, Tom Lau Moon-tong, Wong Wing-Hang, Yongheng Huang, Jiaogao Li and Putang Liu. Action directors[3] were Tony Ching Siu-tung, Philip Kwok Chung-fung, Lau Chi-ho, Alan Tsui Chung-sun and Bobby Woo Chi-lung. Released: July 18, 1987.

In the cast were Leslie Cheung Kwok-wing, Joey Wong Jo-yin, Wu Ma, Lau Siu-ming, Lam Wai, Xue Zhilun, Wong Jing, Huang Ha, Yeung Yau-cheung, Shut Mei-yee, Elvis Tsui and David Wu Tai-wai. The budget was HK $5.6 million (= US $650,000). It was showered with awards (including Fantafestival Rome, Fantasporto Porto Film Festival, and Avoriaz Fantastic Film Festival, and Hong Kong Film Awards for best score, best song and best art dir.), took HK $18.8m gross, and it ran for a blissful 98 minutes.

A Chinese Ghost Story is very much in the same mold as *The Bride With the White Hair* and similar Hong Kong films. It's a romantic tale couched in horror/ fairy tale/ fantasy movie packaging, an impossible romance between a human man and a supernatural woman.

Tsui Hark produced *A Chinese Ghost Story*, and his stamp is all over it: he was involved in developing the project, in creating the script, in the casting, in the visual effects, etc (as Tsui remembered: 'actually, I was thinking of [directing] all of them!'). It was produced by his Film Workshop company (with Cinema City), and his Cinefex Company created the visual effects. The frenetic pace is clearly something close to Tsui's filmic sensibility. It's safe to say that *A Chinese Ghost Story* is very much a Tsui Hark concept (and production). However, he says that it was Tony Ching Siu-tung who directed it, and that he helped out, and directed some parts. As well as Ching's contribution as director, it's also worth noting that the screenplay credit goes to Yuen Kai-Chi: one of the reasons that this movie is so good is because of the brilliant script.

A Chinese Ghost Story marks the first of the really great Tsui Hark and Tony Ching Siu-tung movies: no doubt about it, the two trilogies – the *Chinese Ghost Story* and the *Swordsman* films – are among the finest in fantasy and action cinema, and one of the greatest collaborations in the history of cinema between a film director and a film producer (see my book on Tony Ching).

It's not bad going, either, for Tony Ching to have a masterpiece as his third film as director – and a much-loved film, too (altho' some critics, including me, would count *Duel To the Death* as a masterpiece, too). Thus, Ching is the man behind not one but two greatly admired and enjoyed series of films – *A Chinese Ghost Story* and *The Swordsman*.

Tsui Hark said that Ching Siu-tung had been reluctant to accept the directing assignment, partly because his previous movie, *The Witch From Nepal*, which also had supernatural and fantasy elements, hadn't done well at the box office. Ching wasn't feeling great about helming another movie, including one which was a romantic story. As they continued to talk, Tsui said, Ching eventually agreed to do it.

---

3 Jin Guo, Zhilong Hu, Zhihao Liu and Zhongxin Xu are also credited as martial arts directors.

A Chinese Ghost Story was important in Tony Ching's career because it was a hit – his pet project, Duel To the Death, hadn't set the box office aflame, and The Witch From Nepal had fared poorly, too. But A Chinese Ghost Story did great business.

According to Tsui Hark, A Chinese Ghost Story went through some reworking: after the film had shot for some 30 days, and had been cut together, they looked at it and decided that it needed more elements in certain areas. The ending, for instance, was revamped: Tsui, with his producer's hat on, decided that the movie required something bigger. (And yet the giant battle between the Tree Demon and our heroes would be plenty for many movies. A Chinese Ghost Story, however, is definitely Something More).

THE PRODUCTION.

A Chinese Ghost Story was based on the 17th century (Ming Dynasty) stories (found in Strange Stories From a Chinese Studio)[4] by Pu Songling (Pu-Sing Ling, 1640-1715), known as 'Master Liaozhai', tho' much altered (Liaozhai lies behind the Chinese horror tradition).[5] Songling's stories are all about the human body (which makes them perfect for Chinese action movies, which foreground the body constantly), about keeping the body intact (for reincarnation), and about ghosts/ spirits seeking bodies for reincarnation. (Tsui Hark had considered a movie based on Pu Songling's works since 1978; he had pitched it to T.V.B.). The movie changed Pu Songling's stories – to the point where it didn't look much like the original, Tsui commented (LM, 75).

The 1987 movie also references ghost stories from Japan (such as Ugetsu Monogatari (1953), and is a remake of The Enchanting Shadow (Li Hanxiang, 1960), which gave A Chinese Ghost Story its title). Dragon Gate Inn (1967) and Legend of the Mountain (1979) might also be influences (certainly when Tsui Hark came to direct movies such as the Once Upon a Time In China series and The Blade, the nighttime scenes especially have a Chinese Ghost Story feel).[6] Forerunners such as the wonderful Sammo Hung comedy horror flick Spooky Encounters (1980) are also in the mix.

Chinese ghost stories pivot around the theme of reincarnation, and Hong Kong horror movies are defined by ghost stories. It's the *whole body* that's important in the Chinese philosophy of reincarnation (as in Ancient Egyptian religion). Thus, shape-changing or missing limbs is not good, and the body must remain intact (so that decapitation is a major setback, because it means no reincarnation).

The female ghost is one of the principal characters of the Chinese ghost story: typically, the woman is young and unmarried (so that she has no son or husband to burn incense and give offerings so she can find a

---

[4] The stories have also been published as: Strange Tales From Liaozhai, Strange Tales From the Liaozhai Studio, Strange Tales From Make-do Studio and Strange Stories from the Lodge of Leisure.
[5] For Chinese audiences, the beliefs and superstitions presented in horror movies aren't fake: 'Hong Kong horror films reflect the genuine beliefs and fears of a superstitious people', pointed out Bey Logan (101). They were also the basis for A Touch of Zen (1971).
[6] Hong Kong critics said that A Chinese Ghost Story looked like a TV commercial; quite a few movies of the 1980s drew on this look (as well as pop promos and MTV).

decent spot in the after-life). The female spirits search for the romance among the living that they didn't experience when they were alive. So that Chinese ghost stories tend to be romances, between human men and ghostly women. Two figures usually crop up as well: the Taoist monk, who tries to protect the man from the ghost (and from his own earthly desires), and a demon or monster, who wants the ghost for itself.[7]

The female ghost or spirit is a *juli*, a seductress, and sometimes a *xian*, a fairy (she is usually beautiful, proving the necessary eye candy, and also suggesting 'she was a victim of a love that went wrong').[8] The man tends to be an effete, harmless, goofy guy.

There were two sequels to *A Chinese Ghost Story*, as well as the inevitable quick cash-ins from rival Hong Kong film teams. In *Portrait of a Nymph* (a.k.a. *Picture of a Nymph*), for instance, released the following year (1988), some of the same cast (including Joey Wong and Wu Ma), run thru exactly the same story (some folk prefer it to *A Chinese Ghost Story*). As a partial tribute to Leslie Cheung Kwok-wing, *A Chinese Ghost Story* was re-released in a restored version in 2011 (and there was a special screening, which cast and crew attended).

The *Chinese Ghost Story* sequels added cast members such as Jacky Cheung (another pop music icon in China). Cheung, one of the four Canto-pop stars (and dubbed 'the King of Canto-pop'), is wonderful in *A Chinese Ghost Story 2*, and also appeared in many other movies in this period, including action thrillers (such as *Bullet In the Head*), and Tsui Hark's films, such as *Wicked City*. Meanwhile, Tony Leung Chi-wai took over Leslie Cheung's role for the second *Chinese Ghost Story* sequel of 1991. A remake of *A Chinese Ghost Story* (a.k.a. *A Chinese Fairy Tale*), was produced in 2011 by Golden Sun Films.

In 1987, when the top-grossing movies around the world were *Fatal Attraction, Beverly Hills Cop 2* and *The Living Daylights*, *A Chinese Ghost Story* is a hugely enjoyable flick which can compete favourably with anything released that year (or any year). For example, the movies in the horror and fantasy genre in the U.S.A. of 1987 included *Predator, RoboCop, The Witches of Eastwick, Nightmare On Elm Street 3, Batteries Not Included, The Lost Boys, Innerspace* and *The Running Man*. Sure, we've all seen all those movies (and enjoyed them!), but *A Chinese Ghost Story* trounces them for imagination, style, wit and action (and beauty – what actors in those North American flicks can compete with Joey Wong and Leslie Cheung?!).[9]

By comparison with North American ghost romance pictures of the same period, such as *Ghost* (1990) and *Always* (1989), *A Chinese Ghost Story* is marvellous. It doesn't have time for anything approaching 'realism' or everyday reality (why bother? you're surrounded with it!). *A Chinese Ghost Story* is a movie-movie that celebrates its movieness with every shot. In *A Chinese Ghost Story*, 'the story of undying love and Good vs. Evil is told in the style of an American horror film on speed', as Lisa Morton

---
7 J. Yang, 2003, 76, 77.
8 S. Teo, 1997, 222.
9 'Where *A Chinese Ghost Story* is way ahead of its American counterparts is in its use of romance and sensuality', noted Lisa Morton (LM, 72).

put it (LM, 72).

A Chinese Ghost Story is a feast of a movie, deliberately corny, popcorny, cheesy, silly, over-the-top, and it doesn't take itself seriously for a second. It's glorious fun, the movie equivalent of a pantomime, or a fancy dress party. The pacing and editing is spot-on: just enough is spent on establishing the hero Ning[10] Choi-san's character, for instance, but not too much; the action scenes are stuffed with beats and gags, but the action is pinned to the central conflicts of each scene, and never allowed to run on simply for the sake of more action, and the 1987 movie has plenty of time to explore the intimate, romantic moments between Ning Choi-san and Nip Siu-shin.

If you rush the slower scenes in your haste to get to more action or more horror, the audience hasn't spent enough time with the characters, or their relationships, or the situations. It is, after all, the *characters* and their *relationships* and the *story* which really make a comedy work. Great comedy comes out of the drama and the characters and the situations (as all of the major comedy filmmakers assert); *A Chinese Ghost Story* follows this all-important tenet (which Tsui Hark wholly understands). But that also applies to great horror movies or great action movies or great romantic movies.

Or put it like this: *A Chinese Ghost Story* has a terrific, cleverly written script that hits all of the right notes at the right time. Oh, it's not *The Cherry Orchard* or *Twelfth Night.* But it's not meant to be! It's a piece of candy, but brilliantly executed.

The script of *A Chinese Ghost Story* is once again constructed along classical lines: act one, for instance, climaxes with the Swordsman Yin versus ghost battle; act two has a similar but bigger conflict between Yin and the monsters, but closes instead with the comical courtroom scene (and Ning Choi-san and Yin agreeing to join forces). The court scene (where Ning reports a murder) lightens the proceedings, providing a farcical breather before the two finales in act three. The court scene is important, too: after it, the relationship of Ning and Yin is cemented: now they are resolved to combat the ghosts and monsters.

As Thomas Weisser put it:

> this is a brilliantly conceived fantasy featuring two very likable Asian performers, Leslie Cheung and Joey Wong. But the real star is Ching Siu Tung and his extraordinary camerawork. (40)

Ric Meyers summed up *A Chinese Ghost Story* thus:

> Ching Siu-tung's splendid fantasy of a thousand-year-old unisex tree demon with a mile-long tongue, pimping a beautiful spirit for 'the big evil'. Sit back – you literally haven't seen anything like this before.[11]

Kozo in Love HK Film reckons that

---

10 Some translations used the name Ling.
11 Quoted in F. Dannen, 373.

the most compelling thing about *A Chinese Ghost Story* is probably its sheer cinematic energy. People fly, jump, and engage in situation comedy with little pause for breath... *A Chinese Ghost Story* is primo eighties Hong Kong Cinema, which means a complete disregard for any attempt at realism. Everything here is so hyperrealistic and over-the-top it makes Hollywood musicals look like the very model of restraint.

THE CAST.

There are three main characters in *A Chinese Ghost Story*:
- Ning Choi-san, the hapless scholar and debt collector
- Nip Siu-shin, the beautiful ghost (*kuei*) of the story
- Yin Chik-ha, the Taoist demon hunter[12]

The cast of *A Chinese Ghost Story* is terrific, headed up two of the most beautiful people in Chinese cinema of recent times: Leslie Cheung Kwok-wing and Joey Wong Jo-yin. You can look at these two lovely actors all day. They are simply sensational. Cheung is especially fine with the comedy in *A Chinese Ghost Story* (always an attribute that's under-valued by film critics), but he's also prime leading man material: Cheung is *hot!*

LESLIE CHEUNG.

Leslie Cheung Kwok-wing[13] was a much-revered star in both the pop music and film worlds. In Asia, pop stars regularly move into movies and television (just as they do in the West). Somehow, the stigma of a rubbish pop idol trying to achieve plaudits in cinema isn't attached to Asian stars – many of the most memorable turns in recent Asian cinema are from pop stars.

Leslie Cheung Kwok-wing was born on Sept 12, 1956 in Hong Kong (his father was a tailor). Sadly, he committed suicide in 2003 by jumping from a 24 storey Hong Kong hotel. He suffered from depression. His suicide note said he'd had enough (altho' he had been seeing doctors). Cheung starred in many movies, some of them first-rate, including *Ashes of Time, A Better Tomorrow 1 & 2* and *Happy Together.* At the time of *A Chinese Ghost Story*, Cheung also appeared in the critically acclaimed *Rouge*, as well as *A Better Tomorrow.* Cheung was often paired with fellow pop star and actress Anita Mui. Cheung's sexual identity was a focus of attention; he dated both men and women, and said it was best to describe him as bisexual (some of his film roles explored his queer media image, such as *Farewell My Concubine* and his films with director Wong Kar-wai).

Educated in England (like many Hong Kong actors), in Norwich and Leeds, Leslie Cheung began his pop singing career in 1977. He worked for the R.T.V. network in Canton (many future stars of Hong Kong cinema started out in television). Cheung gave up singing in 1989[14] to concentrate on acting ('as an actor, you can go much further – travelling back and forth in time, playing different characters. It's like having more lives during your

---

[12] The *fat-si* is a Taoist priest or shaman who has spells and magic to deal with ghosts and spirits. The *fat-si* takes on physical and scientific as well as religious tasks.
[13] Leslie Cheung's name in Cantonese is Jeung Gwok-wink and Zhang Guorong in Mandarin. He is sometimes billed as Leslie Cheung Kwok-wing.
[14] After giving sell-out concerts on 33 consecutive nights at the Hong Kong Coliseum.

lifetime', he explained).15 Cheung later returned to live performance, embarking on several successful tours.

A Chinese Ghost Story is one of Leslie Cheung's most enjoyable performances (he was really hitting his stride at this time – he also delivered a scorching performance in *A Better Tomorrow,* the year before *A Chinese Ghost Story*). Cheung's Ning Choi-san is well-meaning but cowardly, naïve (even simple) and unremarkable. He's the everyday guy hero, the ordinary guy who finds himself in extraordinary circumstances.16 He doesn't want to be where he is, and he wants to stay out of trouble. He's poor, and doesn't like his job, but does it anyway (all attributes that everybody can identify with! Ning is a very Tsui Harkian characterization).

Leslie Cheung is carrying *A Chinese Ghost Story* for long stretches – where he's the only character on screen (for instance, in the earlier scenes which are essentially a guy in a haunted house scenario. And just one guy, not a couple or a group). This is a *tour-de-force* comedy turn: one of the reasons that the *Chinese Ghost Story* films are so effective and so entertaining is down to Cheung's performance.

The 1987 movie also gleefully delivers gender reversals, too – by having Ning Choi-san play a feminized role (to the point where, in the 1990 sequel, he's taking a bath when the monster appears, a cliché of the horror genre, where it's usually an opportunity to see a starlet unclad).

Amazingly, Leslie Cheung looks about 18, altho' he was 30[17] at the time of the first *Ghost* movie (Cheung also plays Ning Choi-san much younger than his real age, 20 instead of 30, but he carries it off). Like Maggie Cheung, Brigitte Lin and Chow Yun-Fat, Cheung is an ageless actor.

JOEY WONG.

Meanwhile, Joey Wong is… Joey Wong! A face that can melt the lens, the 20 year-old Wong Jo-yin (b. Jan 31, 1967, Taipei, Taiwan) needs to do nothing except just stand there to be incredible (tho' she does plenty more'n that in *A Chinese Ghost Story*! Critics unfairly carped that thankfully all Wong has to do is show up; but no, she is acting her socks off too. And she is terrific in other Tsui Hark-related movies, such as *Green Snake* and *The Swordsman 3*).

Joey Wong Jo-yin would later appear as one of the snake-women in *Green Snake* (1993), a movie which's essentially the same plot as *A Chinese Ghost Story*.[18] (Casting the female ghost was probably the toughest casting job in *A Chinese Ghost Story* – finding character actors to play mad, Taoist monks or scary Tree Demons isn't so difficult! But the actress selected to play Nip Siu-shin had to be other-worldly and convince as a ghost, but also be attractive, and a good actor. Sounds easy to find?

---

15 However, Tsui Hark said that Cheung had been reluctant to take on the role, because he'd had bad experiences in playing in period roles (in TV).
16 Lisa Morton describes Leslie Cheung's Ning Choi-san as 'idealistic without being naïve, clumsy without being foolish, romantic without being maudlin, and frightened without being weak' (LM, 73)
17 He's 11 years older than Joey Wong.
18 Joey Wong became a favourite for Tsui – perfectly cast in *The Swordsman 3* and *Green Snake* as doomed, tragic heroines.

Trust me, having done casting myself, it's not that easy! What you find with casting is that if you have five boxes to tick, many actors you see will cover three or four of the requirements, but not all five).

Incidentally, Joey Wong was not Tsui Hark's first choice for the ghost in *A Chinese Ghost Story* – he thought she looked too contemporary and too tall – she's 5' 8" (his choices included Japanese singer Akina Nakamori and May Lo). But when Tsui and the team saw Wong in the costume, it was obvious she was perfect.

Ching Siu-tung wanted Joey Wong and Leslie Cheung for *A Chinese Ghost Story* precisely because they were very contemporary actors: they would revive the genre with new blood. (Ching took the same approach by casting singer and TV actress Kelly Chen in *An Empress and the Warriors*, another of his big, romantic movies).

The actors in *A Chinese Ghost Story* throw themselves into the roles – it's very physical stuff. Apart from the action scenes, the actors're drenched with rain, wading waist-deep in water, close to fire, or falling into the sea (Leslie Cheung gamely does this a number of times – not counting the takes we don't see!). A Chinese action movie is no easy ride for the cast, as many visiting Western performers have found out.

THE SECONDARY CHARACTERS.

And – this is also perfect casting – Wu Ma plays the Taoist monk hunting down the spirits. Wu Ma (1942, Tianjin – 2014), sometimes known as Feng Wuma, is a veteran of literally hundreds of movie appearances (around 250), as well as a prominent film director (he was A.D. to Chang Cheh, and directing from 1970 onwards).[19]

Wu Ma steals every scene he's in. His introduction, for instance, is genius: instead of having Ning Choi-san encounter Yin Chik-ha creeping around the temple at night, or stumbling upon him in the village by day, Ning Choi-san runs into Swordsman Yin in the midst of an epic sword duel with an arch rival, Hah Hau (played by Lam Wai). So, cleverly, the screenwriter (Yuen Kai-Chi) weaves in exposition about the temple and the spirits in the middle of a juicy slice of furious swordplay and wire-work. And we see Yin in his element, at work, *showing* us what he does (instead of him *telling* us about it).

On this same crazy night, the rival swordsman Hah Hau encounters Ning Choi-san in the wilds, in the midst of another swordplay scene; later, the rival swordsman becomes one of the ghost's sorry victims (as he nurses his wounds beside a campfire; Nip Siu-shin materializes as a seductive water nymph, and Hah Hau is soon engulfed in a monstrous tongue and sucked dry).

A Chinese Ghost Story is happy, too, to portray a powerful and predatory woman. Nip Siu-shin is depicted seducing and tupping two victims before she meets scholar Ning Choi-san. However, the movie lets the beautiful ghost stay this side of murder, when the lovemaking scenes cut to a point-of-view, Steadicam shot (the classic, subjective monster

---

[19] Wu Ma has directed movies with similar man-and-ghost romances to *A Chinese Ghost Story*, including *Portrait of a Nymph* and *Burning Sensation*.

shot of 1980s horror cinema) of the thing or monster approaching rapidly. While Siu-shin looks on, it's the monster that does the actual killing (it's not revealed in full until later).

CASTING.

One should also note here Tsui Hark's genius with casting. Rarely commented upon by critics (tho' discussed endlessly by fans), casting is enormously important in a movie. And it's not an easy job. Tsui certainly has a knack for finding new talent, for getting the right people for the roles (he has also created roles specially for certain actors), and also for filling in the secondary roles and the character roles with suitable people. In *A Chinese Ghost Story*, everyone can agree that Leslie Cheung was the perfect choice.

Tony Ching has used many pop stars in his films as film director – the ones produced by Tsui Hark, obviously, but also his more recent works, such as Kelly Chen appearing in *An Empress and the Warriors*, and Xiao Zhan in *Jade Dynasty* (both Chen and Zhan are wonderful, and, being the main characters, they have to be).

ROMANCE AND HORROR.

Nip Siu-shin is enslaved to the Tree Demon, a.k.a. Old Dame (Lao-lao): she is forced to procure men for the Tree Demon by having sex with them: the Tree Demon then rushes in to suck out their energy – with a giant tongue! (presumably their *chi* is high during lovemaking). It's a grotesque version of a sadomasochistic, master-and-slave, pimp-and-prostitute arrangement.

The horror genre aspects are the packaging in *A Chinese Ghost Story*, as Tsui Hark explained, that covers what is really a romance story. Horror and romance would be plenty, but, this being Cantonese cinema at its finest, two other elements're added: action and comedy. Getting the *mix* right is *so* important, and *A Chinese Ghost Story* is perfectly pitched in terms of tone and attitude as well as its balance between action + comedy + romance + horror.

And notice how each element complements the other: there are genuinely creepy moments in *A Chinese Ghost Story* (it is a perfect Hallowe'en movie), but they are always balanced by comedy before and after. The romance, meanwhile, is genuine (there is definitely a chemistry between Leslie Cheung and Joey Wong), but again the humour lightens it (and inevitably interrupts it). Meanwhile, the action, as one might expect, is truly extraordinary – in live-action, Chinese filmmakers have *no competition* from any filmmakers anywhere on Earth.

A Chinese Ghost Story is also the first grand expression of the importance of romance and romantic desire in the cinema of Tony Ching Siu-tung (it was a subplot in his previous two movies as director, *Duel To the Death* and *The Witch From Nepal*). It's surprising just how much romance is a key ingredient in Ching's films, even tho' he's known as one of the premier action directors on the planet. One of the memorable aspects of *A Chinese Ghost Story* is the lovers crying 'Ning Choi-san!' or 'Siu-shiiiin!' to each other.

The romantic plot in *A Chinese Ghost Story* reaches a heightened point in the finale, when the lovers share a final moment together, and then Nip Siu-shin is gone. Forever.

When a movie gets the *balance* between horror and comedy right,[20] it's very satisfying. In *A Chinese Ghost Story*, the filmmakers might have had recent (pre-1987) outings in the U.S.A. such as *Ghostbusters* or *E.T.* or *The Evil Dead* in mind. More recently, the humour in the *Pirates of the Caribbean* series hits a very similar tone (lavish vistas, great visual effects, and spooky moments, but not too gory or nasty – and, at the heart of it, a well-meaning but klutzy guy. In fact, Johnny Depp has affinities with Leslie Cheung, in the way that Depp played Captain Jack Sparrow in *Pirates*. And in the *Chinese Ghost Story* sequel of 1990, when Cheung has his beard and moustache, he's even more Depp-ish).

COMEDY.

A Chinese Ghost Story is very funny. In the bustling village scene (mandatory in any historical movie, East or West, always in the first act), everybody regards Ning Choi-san as a doofus. When he asks about the temple where he wants to spend the night because he's broke, everyone mutters behind his back that he's a dead man, very much in the Mel Brooks mold when someone mentions Dracula's Castle (and Tsui Hark is very fond of such comical crowd scenes). There's some inventive comedy using rain and water: the debt collector's account book is a soggy mess of smeared black ink, and Ning Choi-san has charms against spirits imprinted on his back when he's pushed against a store display (again, it's likely that Tsui Hark was behind these gags).

As so often in Chinese, fantasy movies, there's some pantomime-style crossdressing in *A Chinese Ghost Story*: the Tree Demon, Old Dame, is played by Lau Siu Ming, a veteran of numerous *kung fu* movies (and like many supernatural foes, s/he has an imperious, echoey voice).

And, just as in a pantomime, there is a lengthy comical sequence where the Mother-In-Law From Hell comes to visit: the Tree Demoness pays a visit to Nip Siu-shin's chamber, announcing that she's got to marry the Lord of the Black Mountain in three days. Siu-shin, meanwhile, hides Ning Choi-san in a wooden bathtub (so that the Old Dame can't smell him – this's also why Siu-shin meets her lover out on the water, in the pavillion). Comedy, farce, hiding lovers from stern, parental figures – it's all delightfully silly (Ning catches glimpses of Siu-shin half-dressed... her sister Siu Ching, is on her case... and the Old Dame catches the scent of the human Ning several times). And it's sexy – the moment when the topless Siu-shin leans down into the water to kiss Ning underwater is iconic.[21] And *A Chinese Ghost Story* is absolutely jammed with memorable images like that.

---

20 The humour in *A Chinese Ghost Story* is perfectly pitched – it's very funny, but it doesn't detract from or stop the story, and it doesn't lessen the atmosphere of dread.
21 'One of the loveliest kisses in all of modern cinema' (Lisa Morton 73).

TECHNICAL ASPECTS.

Technically, *A Chinese Ghost Story* is a marvel. The production design, the costumes, the hair, the make-up, the editing, the cinematography, the sound design – all departments are working at their optimum. There is a wonderful use of props, for instance: Swordsman Yin has his anti-demon charms and a magical sword, and much is made of the painting of Nip Siu-shin which Ning Choi-san spots in the village market (that prop does a *huge* amount of narrative work in the first two *A Chinese Ghost Story* movies).[22] Meanwhile, texts and words are everywhere – from the cemetery stones and the wayside markers, to the paper charms deployed by the Taoist monk and Ning's soaked tax account book. There's even time for the lovers to indulge in some Chinese calligraphy during one of their (all too brief) sojourns together.

All of the *Chinese Ghost Story* films, like many historical movies, are costume movies: *A Chinese Ghost Story* is filled with flapping, floating and very long pieces of material (Shirley Chan and Kitty Ho Wai-Ying were the costume designers). Joey Wong Jo-yin, as the chief female star of the movie, receives the most lavish treatment from the hair, make-up and costume departments: Wong's Nip Siu-shin is more a bundle of white or red cloth fluttering in the wind than a former human being now ghost.[23] The movement of the clothes, one of the hallmarks of Chinese, historical movies, perfectly embodies her in-between status, in a limbo between life and death. (In Chinese costume dramas, clothes don't hang statically on the body, they are photographed in motion, which enhances their beauty).

The acting style and the staging in *A Chinese Ghost Story* is inventive and, by Western standards, unorthodox. For example, characters standing and spouting dialogue, the default performance style in Western TV and film, is only part of the mix in *A Chinese Ghost Story*. Just as common are scenes where a character leaps up into a tree, or performs a weepy, emotional scene lying on the floor. The Peking Opera style of performance, beloved of Tsui Hark, is displayed throughout *A Chinese Ghost Story*, and not only in characters such as the Tree Demon and Nip Siu-shin.

Seven cinematographers worked on *A Chinese Ghost Story* (probably more if you count second unit and visual effects teams – and some celebrated names, such as Tom Lau Moon tong, Poon Hang-sang, etc), but the result is completely unified[24] – and absolutely gorgeous. This 1987 movie is a photographic feast, and it's got the lot, technically: lamplight, candlelight, firelight, sunset, dawn, night (many ways of lighting a night scene), lightning, explosions, and visual effects.

The sound editing, mixing and dubbing (by Xiaolong Cheng, David Wu Tai-wai and Qun Xue) on *A Chinese Ghost Story* has had a little more time

---

[22] When Nip Siu-shin's not on screen, it's a reminder of her; Ning sees the picture before he meets Nip; Ning goes back to buy it; it's handed back to Ning by Nip; the art dealer tells Ning Choi-san that the model has been dead a year; it reminds Ning of Nip at the end of act two; Siu-shin tells Ning to keep ahold of it, and it's the only memento of her he'll have; and, yes, he's clutching it in the final scene.
[23] The filmmakers use several techniques to give Siu-shin a gliding, floaty motion.
[24] No matter how many photographers shoot a Hong Kong movie, the results always seem to be in sync.

and energy spent on it than your average Hong Kong movie (in any genre). There are some wild sounds in *A Chinese Ghost Story*: tapping, bubbling sounds for the creatures in the temple; loud, echoing voices for the demons; every variation on whooshes for the swordplay and ærial flights; comical, spooky noises when Nip Siu-shin uses her ghostly magic; and extraordinary screams in the underworld sequence.

The score – by James Wong Jim, Romeo Diaz, David Wu Tai-wai and Dai Lemin – includes the expected traditional, Chinese music, and electronica and breathy synthesizer effects for the supernatural scenes.

Editing orchestrates the boundaries between life and death in *A Chinese Ghost Story*: several times, it's simply a single cut, and not a grand visual effect accompanied by 50 channels of noisy sound effects, that takes someone away (to death) or brings them back (to life). For instance, our heroes pick up a bunch of funeral urns, each containing a ghost. Swordsman Yin asks the ghosts to take their urn and leave – they do, and in a cut to the reverse angle, they have already gone. Similarly, when Nip Siu-shin appears to Ning Choi-san in the inn, there's a cut to the reverse angle and Siu-shin is already there, standing behind the scholar. Finally, in the deeply moving climax of the movie, Nip Siu-shin disappears in between the shots, as the camera stays on Ning and we hear Yin's voice off-screen: 'she's already gone'.

Forget wild (and expensive) visual effects, whooshing sound effects, wreathes of smoke and flashing lights, the most formidable effect in cinema, as all good filmmakers know, is the simple cut. With just one cut, you can create – or destroy – anything.

VISUAL EFFECTS.

A Chinese Ghost Story is another of Tsui Hark's visual effects feasts. The visual effects were delivered by his company, Cinefex Workshop, and overseen by Ma Xian Liang. Altho' the visual effects budget was in the region of $160,000 (!), they are marvellous, because of the way that they are integrated into the storytelling. That is, the $160,000 spent on the visual effects in *A Chinese Ghost Story* was more successful by far than the million$ spent solely on effects in Hollywood blockbusters such as *Snow White and the Huntsman*[25] or *Where the Wild Things Are*. Because those movies reek! And *A Chinese Ghost Story* simply *sings*.

Among the notable visual effects in *A Chinese Ghost Story* are the stopmotion animated creatures, very much in the Ray Harryhausen mold (and marvellously integrated with the live-action). There are also matte shots, miniatures, animation, and optical printing (the movies of Tsui Hark are especially fond of integrating matte paintings with live action, to create those impossible, vast vistas vital to much of fantasy cinema). And, with all those inanimate objects to animate, like giant tongues or swords or tree roots or tentacles, there is a lot of on-set puppeteering in *A Chinese Ghost Story*, plus some animatronics, and special make-up.

---

25 *Snow White and the Huntsman* cost an astonishing $170 million! What a shocking waste of money! Just think what the Chinese film industry could do with $170 million – in 1987 – or now!

Many of the effects were of course created on the set, in front of the camera. *A Chinese Ghost Story* is, like *The Blade* or *The Bride With White Hair*, a fantastically sexy movie in its evocation of *texture* and *atmosphere*. Rain effects, fire effects, smoke effects, lightning effects, wind effects and wire effects – *A Chinese Ghost Story* has got the lot. Every shot has smoke billowing through it (and leaves), wind machines blowing clothing, and, for the lighting, deep blues for the nighttime scenes and reds and orange for the fires and the lamps and the candles.

ACT ONE.
Let's have a look at some of the scenes: –
A Chinese Ghost Story opens with a pre-credits teaser featuring the Chinese ghost of the title, in the form of Joey Wang, preying upon a hapless scholar working at his books late at night (one of those places where the windows are always open, where drapres're always fluttering, where the art direction and lighting are exquisite). The spectre appears outside the room, then moves inside to seduce the scholar. The dreamy atmosphere is enhanced by the flapping, white drapes, and the female voice singing.

Ning Choi-san is introduced travelling on his own through the countryside on his way to collect taxes (a thankless job). The rigours of travel (and Ning's characterization) are evoked with some basic realities of life – food (inedible) • and theft (unavoidable) • and death (instant) • and terrible weather (cold and wet).

Sheltering from a rainstorm, Ning Choi-san finds himself witnessing a savage and bloody running battle, with a swordsman pursing and nobbling several thieves (this is a kind of send-up of Akira Kurosawa's cinema – rain, countryside, swords, sudden violence, etc).[26] The scene evokes the proximity of comedy and violence, which's a recurring feature of the *Chinese Ghost Story* movies.

After delineating Ning Choi-san's characterization and predicament (as a lowly but diligent tax collector), *A Chinese Ghost Story* continues with the marvellous bustling village sequence. It's packed with incidents – selling paper charms,[27] an art dealer,[28] a street brawl, looking for somewhere to stay, finding something to eat, tax collecting, the search for wanted men,[29] the superstitious crowd, and the painting of the ghost.

The rapid shift from day to night[30] takes us into horror movie territory, with Ning Choi-san heading for the Hotel From Hell, the Lan Yeuk Temple, through a forest of wolves. All of the clichés of the horror genre are included with such charm and ingenuity, no one minds if we've seen this hokum 1,000s of times before.

---

[26] Ning might be starving, but after the swordsman's left, he immediately throws the gift of some bread away.
[27] Folklore and superstition are evoked throughout *A Chinese Ghost Story*.
[28] There's a great gag of the art seller turning all of his wares away from onlookers when he discovers that Ning is poor.
[29] The belligerent and dim cops armed with swords looking for the criminals on the wanted posters are a classic running gag (very Tsui-ian). Later, a guy's dragged in who's the spitting image of Swordsman Yin. (Tsui used the gag later, with the impostors in *The Swordsman 3* and *Iron Monkey*).
[30] Via some optical wipes.

The Lan Yeuk Temple is the setting for the introduction of the third major character in *A Chinese Ghost Story*, the Taoist sword master, Swordsman Yin. Once again, Ning Choi-san has the habit of stumbling into trouble; wherever he is, things go wrong. The staging of the scene is masterful, with Ning caught in the frenetic battle between two ancient, fierce rivals, Yin and Hah Hau – he's trapped literally between the two of them, at sword-point. (Here, one of Ning's only weapons – talk – doesn't quite work, tho' Hah Hau storms off in the end).

We're still only part-way through act one of *A Chinese Ghost Story*, because we haven't even got to the nighttime romance yet, or the conflict between Swordsman Yin and the monsters. *A Chinese Ghost Story* doesn't feel rushed, yet it is also racing along at the frantic pace of the city of the Hong Kong itself.

For example, *A Chinese Ghost Story* has time to depict an exposition scene between Ning Choi-san and Swordsman Yin, a scene of Ning bedding down in the Temple, the awakening of the corpses in the attic above, the demise of Swordsman Hah Hau, and the beginning of the romance of Ning and Nip Siu-shin in the waterside pavillion.

A romance between a human man and a spirit woman is a sub-genre of Chinese romance tales (but it's also found in Western folklore and fairy tales – men and mermaids, for instance). In *A Chinese Ghost Story*, it's staged as a highly stylized scene out of a mediæval painting, unreal and dreamy (torches placed in the water as well as in the pavillion is a great touch, and Nip Siu-shin plays a *qin*), but also delightfully comical.

The climax of act one of *A Chinese Ghost Story* is also the finale of both act two and act three, as usual in many movies. That is, it's a conflict between Swordsman Yin and the monsters, with Ning Choi-san caught in the middle (at this point, Ning doesn't quite know who or what Nip Siu-shin is).

Swordsmen and ghosts leaping up trees (and down them, and through them, and around them, and between them), is a form of action that Ching Siu-tung has been delivering for decades. Ching is the King of Forest Fights, of wire-work amongst leaves and branches.

The finale of act one of *A Chinese Ghost Story* is fast and frantic, but also includes several romantic clinches (Ning Choi-san lands atop Nip Siu-shin with his hand on her breasts, a Japanese *animé* joke, for instance), and some crude comedy (Swordsman Yin urinates in the bushes where Ning is hiding).

ACT TWO.

Act two of *A Chinese Ghost Story* repeats many of the elements we've already seen in act one: more romantic scenes btn Ning Choi-san and Nip Siu-shin, more of Swordsman Yin (his comical song), more of Ning in the scary temple (and the undead), Ning in the woods again (now with three lanterns), Nip snaring another victim, etc.

But there are complications – the biggest is Ning Choi-san coming face to face (or to nose) with Old Dame, the Tree Demonness, and her entourage. If the Old Dame isn't enough as a potential problem to overcome, there's Nip Siu-shin's sister Siu Ching (Sit Chi-Lun), who suspects that Nip is hiding something (or someone).

This lengthy sequence, where Ning Choi-san is hidden by Nip Siu-shin in a bathtub, is played chiefly for laughs (there are many bits of actorly business, as Ning is nearly-but-not-quite-discovered, taking *A Chinese Ghost Story* into romantic farce or comedy of manners territory. Tsui Hark (likely the creator of this part of the film) had already delivered variations on this sort of scene in both *Shanghai Blues* and *Peking Opera Blues*).

But there's also barely suppressed aggression, too. For ex, Old Dame whipping[31] her daughter Nip Siu-shin (and it's not the first time that Nip has been punished). We also see the monsterish side of the Tree Demonness, with glimpses of the giant tongue (tho' the two aren't put together in a single shot yet).

Comedy, aggression – and romance (the first time that the lovers kiss is when Nip Siu-shin gives Ning Choi-san air under water in the tub (a bath scene in movies is also often an excuse to have the lead actress undressing, as here, and kissing under water to give someone air is a common motif. Tony Ching used it recently in *Jade Dynasty*, 2019).

In the resuming of the romantic scenes, Nip Siu-shin and Ning Choi-san consummate their love in the water pavillion, filmed, as always with the pavillion scenes, with drapes fluttering in front of the camera. There's a second song here (following Yin's Taoist song), which turns the love scene into a montage of the lovers' courtship (and a 'Story So Far' summary of the film).

This is a very common narrative device in Hong Kong movies, where an ecstatic moment is riven with evocations of nostalgia and sadness. The lovemaking in the present tense seems overwhelmed by memories, set to a melancholy tune ('Let the Dawn Never Come', sung by Sally Yeh). The song and the montage editing transforms the present moment into a sum of the past, turns lovemaking into memory, and reminds us that although this is sort of the happiest of times, it is also the saddest, because the lovers cannot stay together.

The romance in *A Chinese Ghost Story* has, after all, one of the biggest obstacles you can imagine between two lovers: one of them is dead. They're not from rival clans, not from different social classes, but separated by death.

Hence the bitter poignancy of the scene at the end of act two, when Ning Choi-san and Swordsman Yin visit the cemetery, and Ning confronts the cold, hard fact by the light of day: Nip Siu-shin's gravestone, with her name on it. These are tried and tested ingredients of folklore, bringing together love and death, and they always work.

---

[31] The whip neatly links to the giant tongue.

ACT THREE.

A Chinese Ghost Story isn't content with one finale: it has two! And both *rock*, big-time. Indeed, *A Chinese Ghost Story* has a final act as stupendous as any other movie ever made. The ending of *A Chinese Ghost Story* is a *tour-de-force* of filmmaking; it features a barrage of practical effects and visual effects which overwhelm the audience with thrills and invention. As a series of gags and ideas, the final act of *A Chinese Ghost Story* is truly remarkable – but these are not just effects for the sake of effects, they are all tied to the storytelling. And yet, they are not the true ending and resolution of the whole movie: that occurs in the scene in the inn, over two or three close-ups of three people in a room.

The finales of *A Chinese Ghost Story* incorporate every trick and visual effect in film history – pixillation, puppeteering, optical printing, superimpositions, slow and speeded-up film, animation, animatronics, special make-up, and wire-work.

And let's not forget the editing (by David Wu Tai-wai), which cuts the ending within an inch of its life, yet gives everything its proper weight and place, and doesn't shred it with pointlessly rapid editing (as so many other movies do). The two finales of *A Chinese Ghost Story are* cut very fast (as usual in a Tony Ching and Tsui Hark movie), but the pace is in sync with the storytelling and the performances.

In the first half of the finale of *A Chinese Ghost Story*, the Taoist monk Yin Chik-ha and the hapless scholar Ning Choi-san go up against the dreaded Tree Demon, Old Dame. What are they fighting for? Why, the luscious Nip Siu-shin, of course! Only she just happens to be a ghost! (But by this time, Ning has promised Siu-shin that he'll make sure her spirit is laid to rest, which involves digging up her remains in a nearby grave. Swordsman Yin is resistant to the notion: ghosts and humans do not mix, he reckons. But Ning, realizing at last that Siu-shin is a supernatural creature (she acknowledges this to his face), and there's no hope they could be together for long, does the right thing, as a romantic die-hard).

A well-meaning but useless scholar, a crazy, old, Taoist monk, an out-size Tree Demon villain (who has the longest tongue[32] in history), and a beautiful princess who's dead – ahh, it can only be a Chinese, fantasy-action-comedy-horror-romance movie based on a 17th century tale and centuries of superstition and folklore.

◆

The first finale of *A Chinese Ghost Story* would be enough to cap any movie (but the filmmakers, looking at what they'd shot later, opted to go back and add some more). It's centred around the Lan Yeuk Temple, but also takes in much to-ing and fro-ing to the water pavillion (where Ning Choi-san and Nip Siu-shin tryst), and running around the woodland, with occasional visits to an over-grown cemetery (all set at night, of course, with blue lighting, smoke, wind, and flickering flames). The action is spellbinding, with the visual effects, the stunts, the flashing swords, the explosions, and the wire-work coming thick and fast. It's fantastically

---
[32] That tongue is 'horror and high camp, kung fu and special-effects fantasy, it is hyperactive, pathological and multi-dimensional', noted Stephen Teo (1997, 228).

furious fantasy filmmaking, one of those set-pieces where the moviemakers chuck in everything they can get hold of, not caring whether it looks 'real', whether it's 'believable', or whether it even makes sense! Who cares? It's simply sublime!

But, folks, this is not miraculously achieved action and visual effects for the sake of it – the filmmaking is always telling a story, is always dramatizing the struggles between the four protagonists: the young scholar Ning Choi-san who just wants to save Nip Siu-shin and be with her (and help her achieve a peaceful quieting of her restless spirit); the Taoist demon-buster Yin Chik-ha, who wants to vanquish the monsters for once and for all; Siu-shin who hopes that her soul can be laid to rest (and be free of enslavement to the Tree Demon), but also to be with her lover; and the fiendish monster Tree Demon, who wants to slaughter anyone who opposes it (and who won't let Siu-shin go without a fight!).

The scenes in *A Chinese Ghost Story* of the colossal tongue slithering around the temple so it envelops it are brilliant updates of schlocky, 1950s monster movies. There's a Wall of Tongue out there! ('Don't let it get in your mouth!' the heroes yell at each other. Damn right! No French kissing with that demon!).[33] Once the tongue's inside the building, the gags and stunts are amazing – amazingly *rapid*, too, and very funny (As director Ching Siu-tung explained, it took a *lot* of work to make that giant tongue look good. But it was worth it).

As a sequence of in-front-of-the-camera practical effects, this is one of the finest in all cinema, worthy of the maestros of German silent cinema like F.W. Murnau or Fritz Lang. There is the same energetic, try-anything spirit of 1920s German cinema, and the levels of imagination and skill on display are astounding.

Yes, when it comes to puppeteering an entire environment, with breakaway props, walls, floors, ceilings, rafters, tables, windows, balconies and pillars, Hong Kong cinema has no equal. It's as if Hong Kong action cinema is always part-animation, but these guys are animating real things, not drawings or pixels – *whole buildings* as well as people and props and monsters!

Anything can move in Hong Kong action cinema – and frequently does. You thought that chair was just going to sit there quietly throughout the scene? No, Jackie Chan is going to spin it, bounce it to and fro on a victim's head, and then break it over him. You thought that at least the walls might survive intact – no, that giant tongue is smashing through them.

The filmmakers of *A Chinese Ghost Story* also deliver inventive variations on the monster that can transform – so they are throwing tentacles at the audience, then roots that wriggle along (and under) the ground, then branches that leap at the hero, then a giant beak, and even then the monster doesn't – won't, can't – die (another horror movie staple).

The creature is slithering into and out of a hole, sliding under the ground, grasping Yip Siu-shin, and Ning Choi-san, and the Swordsman (at

---
33 We've already seen a ghostly point-of-view shot of the tongue entering a victim's body and sucking the life out of it.

different times), and performing impossible transformations. The filmmakers worked tirelessly to make a giant tongue appear as a fearsome opponent, and they succeeded. It's ridiculous – a giant tongue! Everyone knows that, but one of the tricks in making it work was to approach the whole thing with just the right tone and attitude (the *tone* of *A Chinese Ghost Story* I reckon is absolutely perfect). Thus, there are comical touches, but not too many (the threat is not deflated with laughter); the humour is delicately balanced with the thrills and suspense.

So Swordsman Yin is comically covered with goop but he could still die at any moment. So Ning Choi-san is desperately trying to avoid the tip of the tongue entering his mouth in a humorous manner, but it looks like he might lose.

✦

The second finale of *A Chinese Ghost Story* starts when the heroes visit a new locale, another inn. Here the lovers are re-united (following some business with the multiple funeral urns, which contain ghosts of young women, sort of Nip Siu-shin's sisters. This is played for both comedy and pathos). There are some sweet touches, too – such as Swordsman Yin's embarrassment when he sees the lovers together.

The second finale in *A Chinese Ghost Story,* producer Tsui Hark explained, came about when the filmmakers decided what they had initially scripted wasn't satisfying (the script went thru a number of variations). As they didn't have the $$$$$ for a Big Set (where most action movie finales take place – often it's the super-villain's lair, which is destroyed at the end), they decided they could put the climax in a spaceless space. That is, just a piece of ground (at night, of course), which, with the aid of *tons* of smoke and clever lighting (and slow motion, and a battery of visual effects), they could persuade the audience that it was the underworld (of course, audiences can be easily persuaded: if an actor tells them they're in the underworld, the audience believes it. There's no point *not* buying into it – especially this late in the movie. And, anyway, who knows what the underworld looks like?).

There are so many imaginative ideas erupting all over the place in the second finale of *A Chinese Ghost Story*, it's impossible to cite them all. Many of the images and beats are memorable: the running, galloping army that's transparent (carrying Nip Siu-shin in a palanquin[34] to her wedding)... Swordsman Yin kicking Ning Choi-san to soar over the army towards Siu-shin (a p.o.v. shot shows him flying over the army below)... the skull motif – the skulls in the inn, and the mountain of skulls that the Black Mountain Demon stands on... Siu-shin and Ning Choi-san flying through the air, as she rescues him yet again... Ning and Siu-shin crashing into a cliff and being engulfed by clutching arms... Yin taking on the whole army single-handed (and later with a sword crackling with energy)... Yin writing heaven and earth spells on his palm in blood and firing them at the enemy... the Black Mountain Demon's knight disappearing and re-appearing behind Swordsman Yin's back... the screaming heads that shoot out from under-

---

[34] Tony Ching is very fond of galloping palanquin scenes – they appear in his first film, *Duel To the Death.*

neath the Black Mountain Demon's cloak, hurling at Siu-shin and biting her...

The *confidence* of the filmmakers, their *invention* and *creativity*, and the *joy* they have in entertaining the audience, are very infectious in *A Chinese Ghost Story*. You can't help but be blown away by it, swept along by it, and energized by it. The *spirit* of this movie, its *tone* and *attitude*, are so appealing (sometimes you can't believe just how many marvellous scenes the film team have produced in *A Chinese Ghost Story* – but the montage of the movie's highlights that plays over the end credits reminds you, while Leslie Cheung sings the theme song).

And there is a *genuine* feeling of movie magic in *A Chinese Ghost Story* – of filmmakers who're delighting in the magical effects that cinema can create, just like Géorges Méliès was over-joyed like a child when he discovered what movies and cameras could do back in the early 1900s (Méliès would've utterly *adored A Chinese Ghost Story*! This is a Mélièsian movie if ever there was one!).

✦

Let's look at the climactic scene in the inn, when our heroes make it back from the underworld after the battle with the monsters and demons and army of the dead – how they crawl out of thin air into the shadowy interior of the temple just before sunrise (a special effect very reminiscent of *The Wizard of Oz*, *The Invisible Man* or *Stairway To Heaven*). Look at the staging of the scene – how the three actors are exhausted, on the floor,[35] until Ning Choi-san moves to the window, where the sun is streaming in (sunlight is fatal to Nip Siu-shin, like a vampire). Ning can't bear to turn to look at Siu-shin, because he knows he's got to say goodbye to her forever. He faces the window and the light, turned away, and tells her to return with her ashes. A final medium shot of Siu-shin lying on the floor... Then there's a brilliant use of off-screen dialogue, and a cut – when Yin Chik-ha says, 'she's already gone'. And in the blink of an edit made on 35mm celluloid, it's over, the romance is ended.[36]

This scene, not the giant battle in the underworld, resolves the primary plot of *A Chinese Ghost Story* – the love story. Notice how poignant it is, how effective, and how economical – it's played largely over close-ups of the principal actors. And notice too that it's very short, and all the more emotional for it. Many comparable movies, especially in the 21st century, would milk and milk that scene. I find the ending very moving – partly because we are mourning the loss of a much-loved star, Leslie Cheung.

Parts of the window's wooden blinds crumple, letting more light in – the human-and-ghost romance has ended (as it has to), but the light caught on film says otherwise: it is a rich, juicy, orange light, so vibrant you could bathe in it. It's the light of morning: there's no need to draw attention to the countless symbols that the light of sunrise embodies. And *A Chinese*

---

[35] A previous conversation btn the lovers was also played on the floor – in the midst of the giant tongue attack.
[36] The movie closes with our heroes galloping away under a rainbow (several Hong Kong action movies of this period close with the heroes on horseback, including *Peking Opera Blues*, *New Dragon Gate Inn* and the *Swordsman* movies).

Ghost Story as a whole doesn't really want or need spiritual or religious or metaphysical interpretations. But they are certainly there if you want to evoke them. (And yet there is something so luscious about the golden light flooding into the inn, and the way that it has been photographed, that's mysterious and sensual. Like many Chinese, fantasy movies, *A Chinese Ghost Story* is in love with light. It's a movie which uses light itself as a primary dramatic device, like films such as *Close Encounters of the Third Kind*[37] or *Princess Mononoke*).

WE ARE ALL GHOSTS.

There are many poignant moments in *A Chinese Ghost Story*: sure, it's a stops-all-out, fantasy rollercoaster ride, but it also exhibits an acute awareness of issues like time passing and death, like the fleetingness and impermanence of human existence, like the frailty of love and romance. There are scenes in *A Chinese Ghost Story* where the headlong rush of the narrative halts, for instance: such as when Taoist monk Yin Chik-ha has a crisis of conscience, and wonders what the hell he's doing (remarking that he's set himself outside of life, but he's not a ghost, either: he's lost somewhere in-between. To humans, he deliberately appeared as a ghost, but when he's among ghosts, he is the human who wants to vanquish them).[38]

And there's time for a jokey courtroom scene: Ning Choi-san is beaten on the floor while the judge and his assistant berate him (the assistant's played by one of the movie's composers and a major creative talent in Hong Kong cinema, David Wu Tai-wai, and the judge is Wong Jing, one of the moguls of Cantonese cinema).

A Chinese Ghost Story also has time in its jam-packed 98 minutes for some musical montages. There's a delightfully bonkers scene where Swordsman Yin delivers a musical rap about Taoism ('Dao, Dao, Dao, Dao!') as he performs a marvellous sword dance (a set-piece also in the 1960 film). As the lovers make love, we have the customary slow ballad ('Let the Dawn Never Come' by Sally Yeh) playing over close-ups of two beautiful people, Leslie Cheung and Joey Wong. In many a movie, these MTV-a-like[39] montages of lovemaking and togetherness have no dramatic or emotional heat at all, but in *A Chinese Ghost Story* they are delicious.

Because we are all ghosts.

Because we are all here for a moment, then we're gone.

A great fantasy movie, like *A Chinese Ghost Story*, can evoke those spiritual issues so magically, exploring them, yet somehow also offering a kind of emotional/ religious catharsis.

This is great storytelling.

---

37 The deep orange of the sunlight recalls the ball of light on the other side of the door that the child Barry opens in *Close Encounters of the Third Kind* (1977). When he was asked to provide an example of a 'signature shot' or 'master image' in all of his films, Steven Spielberg chose the shot in *Close Encounters of the Third Kind* of the bright orange UFO light outside: 'that beautiful but awful light, just like fire coming through the doorway. And he's very small, and it's a very large door, and there's a lot of promise or danger outside that door'.

38 In *A Chinese Ghost Story*, one of the Taoist swordsman's tasks is to keep the world of ghosts, the *yin*, separate from the world of humans, the *yang*.

39 Ching Siu-tung said the design of *A Chinese Ghost Story* was 'like watching a Chinese MTV'.

A Chinese Ghost Story (1987), this page and over.

倩女幽魂

青山寸寸熟華年
對月形單望相護
只羨鴛鴦不羨仙

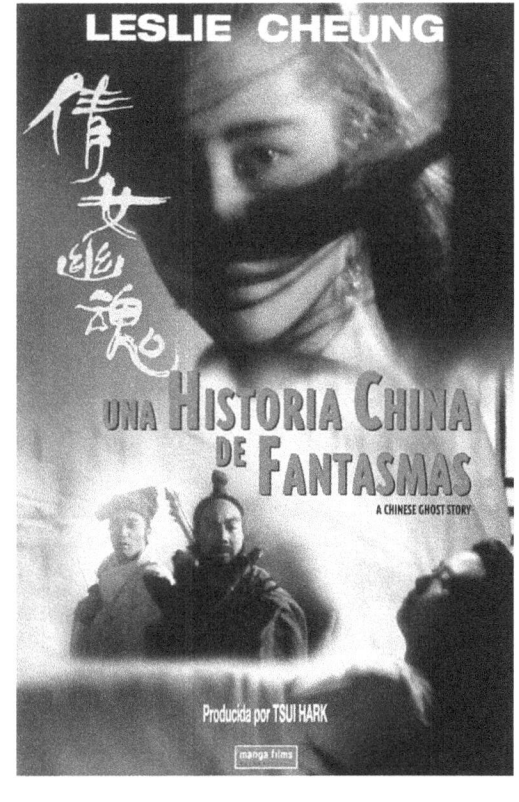

A Chinese Ghost Story film posters.
(This page and over).

2

A CHINESE GHOST STORY 2

Sin Nui Yau Wan II – Yan Gaan Do

Most of the principals of the first *A Chinese Ghost Story* movie returned for the first sequel, including the director, producer and stars. *A Chinese Ghost Story 2* (1990, *Qiannü Youhun Zhi Renjian Dao* in Mandarin = *Sien Female Ghost II: Human Realm Tao*) was written by Lau Tai-mok, Lam Kei-to and Leung Yiu-ming (with a story co-credit for Tsui Hark and Yuen Kai-Chi), with the same cast (Leslie Cheung Kwok-wing, Joey Wong Cho-yin, Wu Ma, and Lau Siu-ming), plus newbies Jacky Cheung (as Chi Chau/ Autumn), and Michelle Reiss (a.k.a. Li, as Yuet Chi/ Moon.) Also in the cast were: Ku Feng, Waise Lee Chi-hung, Lau Shun, Wong Fue-chun, Do Siuy-chin, Johnny Koo, Fei Sing, Wong Hung and Ng Kwok-kin. (Ching Siu-tung directed all three *Chinese Ghost Story* movies, and Tsui Hark was producer on all three). DP: Arthur Wong, editor: Marco Mak Chi-sin, art dirs.: William Chang Suk-Ping and Ho Kim-Sing, sound: Miu Gik Luk Yam Sat, Kwok Wing-Kei, Lam Wing-Cheung and Wong Choh-Keung, costumes: Kitty Ho Wai-Ying, hair: Chau Siu-Mui and Peng Yen-Lien, music: James Wong Jim, Romeo Diaz and Tang Siu-Lam, special fx by Nick Allder and David Watkins, make-up: Man Yun-Ling, and the action dirs. were Cheung Kan Chow, Ching Siu-tung, Bobby Woo Chi-lung, and Lau Chi-ho. Released in July 13, 1990. 98/ 104 minutes.

Produced for around HK $7 million (= US $1 million)[1] – an impossibly tiny budget! – *A Chinese Ghost Story 2* is a typical sequel: More Of The Same, tho' slightly different (however, it develops the Chinese ghost plot into the future, rather than, like many sequels, and most in Hong Kong cinema, re-hashing the same elements but with a new yarn). The first movie was a ghost story and romance; the second focusses on more human issues, or morals and ethics.[2] Altho' film critics made their usual complaints about *A Chinese Ghost Story 2* being less successful than the

---
[1] Bey Logan reckoned the budget was US $7 million, but that seems too high; it might stem from the confusion between Hong Kong and North American dollars. In fact, the first movie cost $650,000, so a step up to $1 million seems correct.
[2] There were many meetings, Tony Ching recalled, as they decided what to do in the *Chinese Ghost Story* sequel.

first movie, I'm sure it played well with viewers (I bet an audience in a multiplex theatre in Kowloon in 1990 enjoyed the scares, the jokes, the romance and the swordplay. It's a perfect Friday Night Movie). After all, you get more Leslie Cheung Kwok-wing (and that's enough for many fans!), and you also get more Joey Wong, and you get Jacky Cheung, and you get Wu Ma! What's not to like?!

Like many sequels, *A Chinese Ghost Story 2* not only draws on the first film in every way, it quotes directly from it, in the form of several montages. *A Chinese Ghost Story 2* opens, for instance, with a montage of images which summarize the story of the first outing. In the middle of act two, to evoke the tragic romance of Ning Choi-san and Nip Siu-shin, there's another montage, which includes the iconic scene of the underwater kiss. Joey Wong sings on the score, along with a female chorus.

✦

Altho' Tsui Hark, among others, were part of the high-powered team of collaborators working on *A Chinese Ghost Story 2*, this is still a Tony Ching movie. And not only in the action scenes: many of the romantic scenes in *A Chinese Ghost Story 2* are far more indulgent, stylized and dreamy than those in the work of Tsui. *A Chinese Ghost Story 2* doesn't feature just one image of the lovers in a close embrace, but many. Often these're filmed in slow motion, with exaggerated lighting. Backlit, floating, the lovers drift across the set or have their faces pressed together on the ground. The camera lingers long over the incredible faces of Joey Wong and Leslie Cheung (and Michelle Reiss).

Ching Siu-tung's cinema pushes romantic motifs into extreme stylization, holding on slow motion images of the lovers far longer than similar movies. The *mise-en-scène* is intricately art-directed, carefully composed, meticulously costumed, with perfect make-up and exquisite lighting. These images have had a lot of time and energy expended in staging them.

✦

Technically, *A Chinese Ghost Story 2* is absolutely amazing: with the legendary Arthur Wong heading up the photography department, this is one of the most ravishing looking of all Hong Kong movies. A huge proportion of the show occurs at night or dusk, requiring a massive amount of lighting equipment. And as it's a historical fantasy, there is plenty of opportunity for highly stylized lighting schemes.

It wasn't easy, though: Arthur Wong recalled an incident on this movie:

> I was hanging from a big crane set above a 100-feet deep cliff. I had to move away from the edge. But they wrongly calculated my weight and when I was in the harness, with the camera and the batteries, I was too heavy. When I just took off, I was upside-down, head down. Wow, it was very scary. And it was very hard to get me back once I was upside-down. People had to come to the edge of the cliff and grab me.
> (D. Vivier)

All of the departments in charge of the visuals are stellar: costumes by Kitty Ho Wai-Ying, hair by Chau Siu-Mui and Peng Yen-Lien, make-up by Man Yun-Ling and art direction by William Chang Suk-Ping and Ho Kim-Sing (many of whom worked for Tony Ching and Tsui Hark on other productions).

The editing of *A Chinese Ghost Story 2* keeps the movie in perpetual motion, yet with many opportunities for reflective interludes, and emotional montages. Tsui Hark's regular editor, Marco Mak Chi-sin, cut this film. One of the chief reasons that *A Chinese Ghost Story 2* is so satisfying is because it is so well-edited.

Finally, the score, by James Wong Jim, Romeo Diaz and Tang Siu-Lam, should be cited as a key ingredient in the success of *A Chinese Ghost Story 2*: as with the *Once Upon a Time In China* films, *A Chinese Ghost Story 2* employs a traditional, Chinese score in the main. As it's also a fantasy movie and a horror movie, however, it uses electronica for suspense. Also, there are several songs in *A Chinese Ghost Story 2*, sung by Leslie Cheung, Joey Wong and a chorus.

✦

One of the delights of a sequel is seeing how the filmmakers employ the elements of the previous movie/s. In *A Chinese Ghost Story 2*, these included finding inventive ways of bringing back props like the painting of Nip Siu-shin, or using the charms, or the demon fights, or the eye candy (male and female) and semi-nude bathing scenes.[3] But a sequel doesn't usually change *everything*, if it's got sense (if you change too much, it's not a sequel, it's a different movie). The trick with a sequel of this kind of fluffy, commercial, popcorn cinema is to give the audience something that seems 'new' yet is also exactly the same (because that's also what the audience want).

It's a tricky balancing act that inevitably means that you keep many ingredients just the same. So in *A Chinese Ghost Story 2* many of the elements are straight repetitions from the first movie: thus, Ning Choi-san is back as the hapless debt collector with his backpack, arriving in a town on his travels; there's a visit to a haunted house, a creepy night spent there during a storm (with a monster appearing), a rough restaurant, wanted men posters, the painting of Nip Siu-shin, another mad Taoist monk, a procession, an arranged marriage, comical bathing scenes, farcical/ partial nudity scenes, romantic kisses, more battles with monstrous foes, more swordplay, etc.

After all, the filmmakers involved in producing *A Chinese Ghost Story 2* are Hong Kong veterans. They are out-and-out capitalists, experienced showmen who aim to *make money* from their movies. Yes – *money!* So *A Chine$e Gho$t $tory 2* is a wholly commercial proposition. Yes, and once the end credits start to roll, the house lights are already up, and you're being hurried out of your seat to make way for the next showing (common

---

[3] The 1990 movie decided that fans would want to see Leslie Cheung taking a bath. So, in the Righteous Villa, Ning Choi-san pops into a wooden bath which's handily nearby. And that's when the monsters show up, just as in a horror movie when the heroine's taking a shower. It's here too where the rap version of *Tao Te Ching* is reprised from the first movie, with Ning singing it now as a protection against evil spirits.

practice in Hong Kong!).

♦

Among the most pressing challenges in *A Chinese Ghost Story 2* was what to do with Joey Wong's character, Nip Siu-shin, who eventually received the peace she desired (a proper death and burial for her soul) in the finale of the first movie. Instead of reviving the character (a cinch to do in a fantasy flick – especially one about life and death and ghosts!), which must've been tempting, the writers and producers opted to have Joey Wong appear as a new character, Windy (who's pretty much the same, of course, but not so wan and pale and ethereal – tho' just as beautiful).

Windy is part of a group that follows Elder Chu – so she is very human, very not-ghostly (but she does have a supernatural moment), and is introduced brandishing a sword which she holds up at Ning Choi-san (thus she is now one of the many female warriors in Hong Kong cinema). They meet following an extravagant nighttime fight scene outside the Righteous Villa, where the rebels dress up as ghosts in white and duel with Autumn (halfway thru act one). This fight scene contains stupendous images – like the would-be ghosts floating down behind Ning.[4] And when Ning catches a glimpse of Windy, he does a double-take, as do we – actors like Joey Wong are literally breathtaking.

A Chinese Ghost Story 2 is a haunted house movie – we spend *a lot* of time in the shadowy Righteous Villa, and far less outdoors, as in the previous *A Chinese Ghost Story* outing. *A Chinese Ghost Story 2* is part comedy horror movie, part *wuxia*/ martial arts movie, part romantic drama, and part farce.

As Windy inevitably falls for Ning Choi-san (and who wouldn't when he's played by the divine Leslie Cheung?!), she agrees at times to pretend to be his lost love, Nip Siu-shin. Ning, meanwhile, spends part of *A Chinese Ghost Story 2* in exhausted or altered states, imagining that Windy is really Siu-shin.

And while Ning Choi-san pines for Nip Siu-shin (even when the wide-awake side of him knows that he'll never see her again – they said farewell forever at the end of the first flick), *A Chinese Ghost Story II* includes a few scenes where both Windy and Moon are looking at Ning lovingly, from afar. The scenes play into the celebrity status of Leslie Cheung, of course – he's the kind of super-babe actor that fans at film premieres scream over. In some scenes in *A Chinese Ghost Story 2*, there isn't even a reverse angle depicting what the women're looking at: instead the camera stays on Moon and Windy, bashing their heads together in their eagerness to try to get a better glimpse of Ning. (As the movie progresses, Moon seems to accept that Ning seems more interested in Windy than her. She sulks and pouts, but in the finale becomes more attached to the Taoist monk Autumn, even tho' this relationship is also doomed. Because when Autumn revives the couple by kissing *chi* back into them, he avoids Moon

---

[4] One of the many marvellous images in *A Chinese Ghost Story 2* features the introduction of the rebels: dressed as ghosts in white, in a forest night scene, they are lowered into the frame out of focus behind Leslie Cheung as if they're corpses hanging from ropes from trees. It's a genuinely creepy image, and the *Chinese Ghost Story* movies are full of such scenes.

because she's a woman. A romance between a woman and a Taoist monk is never going to fly in a Chinese action movie! Even when that monk is played by the appealing pop star Jacky Cheung!).

And *A Chinese Ghost Story 2* is funny. Putting Ning Choi-san in prison with a wily, old coot played by Ku Feng (who's also near-crazy) was a fun skit on *The Count of Monte Cristo* (and the prison genre). Having Ning then being mistaken for Elder Chu, a highly-respected scholar and philosopher, was wonderful (Ning grows a beard in jail, as you do – he's in there for months – so he looks like the Elder. Later, he shaves it off to become the familiar Ning and Leslie Cheung without a beard). In an instant the beardy guise switches the hierarchy of the relationships around, and now Ning is elevated to the leader of the pack, instead of being the rather hopeless youth who's just trying to get along and stay out of trouble. The gag is extended to a scene where Ning shaves off his 'tache, only to find that the rebel group dismiss him as just anyone – without those whiskers, he's a nobody! (Director Ching Siu-tung remarked that he was thinking of Tiananmen Square and the suppression of political rebellion in the personality of Elder Chu, a writer who's imprisoned for apparently politically subversive works (which aren't at all).)

Certainly the political/ ideological opinions of the writers, and Tsui Hark, can be heard in the speech that the old man gives in the cell – he mentions that if he writes history, he's accused of criticizing the present, and if he writes fairy tales, he's charged with purveying superstition (i.e., whatever he does as an artist/ writer, the powers-that-be will find some fault with his work). The Communist ideology of Mainland China is critiqued here.

✦

One of the finest scenes in *A Chinese Ghost Story 2* had the group of rebels eavesdropping on Ning Choi-san and Windy talking following their amazing encounter in the forest. Here is the brilliant use of the painting prop – the calligraphy that Ning and Nip Siu-shin performed in the first *A Chinese Ghost Story* movie (and spoke in voiceover), drawn into the painting, is now switched about. Now the rebel group is thrilled to think that Ning is going to recite some amazing poetry, and they get to hear it. Which he does! And lo and behold, the poem contains clues which the rebels decipher as referring to their Master and the water pavilion (it must've taken some time for the screenwriters to work this out! The comedy, complete with group reaction shots, is very Tsui-ian, as is the mistaken identity gag).

Wu Ma only appears towards the end of *A Chinese Ghost Story 2*: instead, it's Jacky Cheung who takes up the role of the crazy, Taoist demon hunter and companion to Ning Choi-san in the adventure. One of the four pop singers known as the 'Four Golden Kings' (along with Leslie Cheung, Andy Lau and Leon Lai), Cheung is terrific in the comic/ action/ sidekick role of the priest Autumn (he has the same charms and protections against the demons, but he can also burrow under the ground at speed – one of the ninja techniques that Tony Ching is fond of). Cheung gets the tone of these movies spot-on, revelling in the OTT masquerade of it all (*A Chinese Ghost Story 2* is like a Chinese *Abott and Costello* picture – tho' certainly made with more visual panache!). A year later, Cheung was back in a comical role for Tsui Hark, as 'Buck Tooth' So in *Once Upon a Time In China,* and after that in *Wicked City*.

◆

The script of *A Chinese Ghost Story 2* is dense with subplots: the romance between Ning and Windy; the erotic triangle of Ning, Windy and Moon; the romantic rivalry between Windy and Moon; Moon's fondness for Autumn; the Imperial persecution of Windy's father, Lord Fu; the mistaken identity of Ning as Elder Chu; the conflict between the rebels and the government; Official Hu realizing the Imperial court is corrupt; the introduction of the High Priest and his lackeys, and so on.

Multiple identity is another theme in *A Chinese Ghost Story 2* – Ning Choi-san is mistaken for Elder Chu by the rebels (despite his protestations); Windy isn't Nip Shui-sin (but Ning wants her to be); and the High Priest turns out to be a demonic Buddha and then a mad monster.

The narrative in the second act of *A Chinese Ghost Story 2* replays many moments from the first *Ghost* picture (act two is the trickiest part of any commercial movie), but you barely notice it. The characters, motifs and scenarios are switched around, but played for similar sorts of comedy, farce, awkwardness, embarrassment, suspense, etc.

The filmmakers, for instance, milk every ounce of thrills and comedy from a bunch of youths trapped inside a haunted house (the Righteous Villa). They squeeze every cent out of the giant monster and its animatronic head (it spooks Ning Choi-san and Autumn, with a series of gags about the freezing palm charm; it startles Windy taking a bath; and it creeps up on Moon. The monster fights continue outside, with the Imperial official taking it on, as well as Autumn. In some scenes, there's a flying monster hand or just the torso attacking the rebel group).

The filmmakers take great delight in dumping a ton of nasty gunk on their beautiful leading lady, with Joey Wong's Windy turning into a demon for some fun visual effects battles reminiscent of *The Exorcist* (1973), until she's kissed back into reality by Ning Choi-san, as the lovers spin and spin in the air. This provides both a supernatural scene for Joey Wong, where she's ghost-like as in the first flick, but she's a nasty spectre who breathes out snakes, and our Movie Kiss between the two main stars, a reprise of the first film, as a series of cuts show Windy becoming more'n more human. At the end, the lovers drift gently to the floor and Ning seems blissed-out – only for Autumn to exchange his *chi* – it's OK for a Taoist priest to perform mouth-to-mouth on a guy, isn't it?

One bathing scene isn't enough. So the filmmakers have their other main star (Joey Wong) undressing and taking a bath (to wash off the goop the prop department have dumped on her). And of course the giant monster is still lurking around. And of course there's French sex farce comedy when Ning Choi-san tries to cover Windy's modesty from the rest of the rebel gang (this is a replay of the scene where the Old Dame appeared in Siu-shin's chambers in the first film). Ning goes to great lengths to preserve Windy's virtue. Woven into this is the romantic rivalry between Windy and Moon.

Another ingredient added to *A Chinese Ghost Story 2* were the cannibal outlaws: Ning Choi-san is hapless enough to stop over at their inn and restaurant not once but twice! Cue images of severed hands and toes mixed in the stew, and a dog with a hand in its maw. Yuk! (One can imagine that this part of the script came from Tsui Hark; he had made much of mad cannibals in *We're Going To Eat You*).

Either you buy into the comedy or you don't – the sex comedy stuff, the French farce stuff, the cannibals stuff, the monster creeping around and nearly-but-not-quite grabbing the heroine stuff, and the women drooling over a man stuff. But you have to admire the light-hearted spirit in which this 1990 movie is delivered: this is a film that knows it's a pile of fluff, and revels in it. It's a Friday night, popcorn and candy and yelling at the screen sort of movie. It's the movie equivalent of a theme park ride, a haunted house ride at the fairground (plenty of Western movies are like this, and some, like *Pirates of the Caribbean* and *The Haunted Mansion*, are even based on theme park rides!).

✦

A new character, an Imperial official, Hu (played by veteran actor Waise Lee), thickens the plot of *A Chinese Ghost Story 2*, arriving at the end of act two – by first pursuing our heroes into the haunted Righteous Villa, then switching ideological sides when he sees how brave they are, and, when he encounters the super-villain High Priest, how corrupt the Imperial circle is. Hu is a thematic character, then – not essential to the central plot, but he exposes the corruption of the Imperial government. *A Chinese Ghost Story 2* was made not long after Tiananmen Square. (Hu is part of an Imperial guard escorting Windy's father, Lord Fu, to his execution; his scene is filmed, once again, at the stony cliffs and dirt track in the New Territories. The scene features Hu going up against the Taoist priest Autumn).

The sequence where Hu enters the High Priest's lair in *A Chinese Ghost Story 2* is genuinely imaginative and chilling: it's a palace arrayed like a court of law lit by flickering torches where Imperial ministers have been kidnapped and eviscerated, so that only hollow husks remain. It's a terrific satire on the 'hollow men' who rule the land – the literal emptiness and nothingness of civil servants and governments. They're not even corpses, they're just shells. (Meanwhile, out back, Hu stumbles into the charnel pits where bits of bodies are heaped, some still partially alive. And three of the heroes have been imprisoned inside red cocoons, presumably the first stage of evisceration. Hu sets them free, which leads to the finale).

✦

The finale of *A Chinese Ghost Story II* has to top the first movie of 1987, as sequels often try to do: it becomes a giant monster movie, when the new villain, the chief Buddhist monk and adviser to the Emperor, the

High Priest, arrives in town. A formidable opponent, a self-righteous religious figure, who hides behind the paraphernalia of organized religion, the High Priest is played by Lau Shun (a Tsui Hark regular – he was Swordsman Zen in *The Swordsman 2,* the aged Asia in *The Swordsman 3,* Wong Fei-hung's father in *Once Upon a Time In China 3*, and appeared in numerous movies of this period). Crossdressing in villains in Chinese fantasy cinema is once again evoked, when the High Priest speaks in a high-pitched woman's voice. However, that's only part of it: the High Priest is also an adept at spell-casting, reciting enchantments in Sanskrit to over-power his rivals.

When the villain turns into a giant, golden statue of the Buddha,5 you know you are wholly within Asian folktale territory – this sort of imagery, with talking statues of gods, simply doesn't appear anywhere in Western cinema. At the climax of a North American action or fantasy movie, no villain would be allowed to turn into Jesus!

In the finale of *A Chinese Ghost Story 2*, the heroes call on the aid of the crazy, old monk Yin Chik-ha from the first *Ghost* movie: Wu Ma makes a very welcome return as Swordsman Yin, from his bolthole in the Lan Teuk Temple from the first film.6

✦

The visuals in the finale of *A Chinese Ghost Story 2* are stupendous – out come the coloured lights, the glowing miniatures and matte paintings, the optically-printed bolts of magic, the smoke and fire practical effects, and actors and stuntmen are flying all over the screen. The camera is often at ground level, hurtling along. The visual effects are wild, with no holds barred: the earth is cracking open, a giant beastie emerges – a centipede!7 – and our heroes take refuge in a magic circle of flying, golden swords. Every possible visual effect and special effect and practical effect is employed, furnishing so many rapidfire gags. There is, as in the first *Ghost* movie, a joyous celebration of the trickery that cinema can conjure up.

For instance, there's a stunning battle against invisible assailants, as Hu the Imperial official duels with the High Priest's henchwomen, who hurtle at him using ninja-ish invisibility (Tony Ching had employed invisible warriors before – it's irresistible to a filmmaker who enjoys the trickery of cinema). The sword fight is a set-piece all of its own, with Hu playing part of it as a one-armed swordsman (a favourite staple of Chinese *wuxia* cinema), when his arm's cut off early on in the fight. There are incredible details in the scene – such as blood spattering out of invisible wounds onto the dirt (but when they're killed, the ninja lose their invisibility, then disappear).

In the same sort of rocky, threatening arena of stones and night that the first *A Chinese Ghost Story* movie used for its finale, *A Chinese Ghost Story 2* has our heroes battling a giant monster. All sorts of inventive

---

5 The orange and gold lighting accentuates the symbolic colours of Buddhism.
6 This is one reason why Windy and Ning Choi-san get separated from the others. They're pursued by the wolves from the first film, where the mere mention of the dread name Lan Teuk Temple has the beasts fleeing.
7 Like something out of William Burroughs, a critic remarked.

beats and twists are concocted to surprise and delight the audience. In one memorable shot, as the monster appears, the ground erupts, forming a wall of broken stones behind our heroes (instead of the usual flames), who're running towards the camera. In another scene, the two Taoist monks, Yin Chik-ha and Autumn, are eaten by the monster (Yin dives in to save Autumn). Trapped in the yucky goop of the monster's belly, Yin reckons that they could separate their spirits from their bodies and flee. It's a suitably magical escape – a *deus ex machina* sort of escape, and a kind of cheat. But within the context of this high-powered, supernatural movie, where life and death are continually being fought over, the filmmakers get away with it. (However, poor Autumn isn't able to return to his body – there's a startling point-of-view shot, with the power and anxiety of a bad dream, when Autumn's semi-transparent spirit flies right over his body lying on the ground, and off into the black sky. Moon hurries after him, but she can't grasp his spirit).

✦

A Chinese Ghost Story II closes with an audience-pleasing happy ending (thus, because Windy isn't a ghost or dead, our couple can be legitimately together). First, there's another elaborate street procession,[8] echoing the one in the first *Ghost* movie, where Ning Choi-san spots Windy parading thru the village. Windy, sporting an elaborate headdress[9] in a covered palanquin,[10] is going (reluctantly) to her arranged marriage (an echo of the finale of the first *Ghost* flick, where Nip Siu-shin was due to wed the Lord of the Black Mountain). Ning, hurrying into the crowd, generously wishes her well (passing his blessing to her via Moon).

Ah, but we can't leave our hero like that, can we?, watching wistfully and mournfully as the heroine is carried away by fate to a marriage she doesn't want. So the filmmakers close the 1990 *A Chinese Ghost Story 2* with a big reunion scene, out on the hills, staged on horseback so they can have that cliché of all movie clichés: the heroes riding off into the sunset.[11]

Everything about this movie has been designed as a crowd-pleaser – the filmmakers want to entertain the audience more than anything. And they succeed! So *A Chinese Ghost Story 2* duly closes with the lovers re-united (and, please, geeks and crrritics, *don't* remind us that Windy isn't Ning Choi-san's true love, that his beloved is really Nip Siu-shin![12] We know that! And, anyhoo – he's going to be dating a flesh-and-blood woman – and she's played by Joey Wong!).

---

8 Filmed on the Shaws' backlot set.
9 Joey Wong in one of her finest incarnations. The image of Wong in the headdress was employed in the marketing of the movie.
10 No one uses palanquins more than Tony Ching in cinema. Maybe Ching simply enjoys the image of a palanquin (or maybe that's how he thinks the film director should be treated on set!).
11 This occurs in several Hong Kong movies of the period.
12 Or that there'll be repercussions from the arranged marriage.

3

A CHINESE GHOST STORY 3

Sin Nui Yau Wan III: Do Do Do

A Chinese Ghost Story 3 (*Qiannü Youhun III Dao Dao Dao*, directed by Tony Ching Siu-tung, 1991) is a visual effects action comedy masterpiece. At a technical level, it is absolutely staggering. Like many Hong Kong movies (even the bad ones!), *A Chinese Ghost Story 3* is perfect fare for a rowdy, Friday night crowd in a cinema in teeming, neon-bright Hong Kong or Macau (its primary audience). *A Chinese Ghost Story 3* makes no pretence at being anything other than a straight-ahead slice of polished, incredibly sophisticated (yet grungey) entertainment. *A Chinese Ghost Story 3* is a winner in every area.

Many of the cast and crew of *A Chinese Ghost Story 3* had worked on the previous installments in the *Chinese Ghost Story* series (this one appeared a year after the second movie). Tony Ching Siu-tung was back directing (and he was one of the action directors, along with Ma Yuk-shing, Yuen Bun and Cheung Yiu-sing; Bruce Law handled the fire and burn stunts); Tsui Hark produced and co-wrote the script with regular collaborator Roy Szeto Cheuk-hon; Cho King-Man co-produced; exec. producers: Chui Bo-Chu and Roger Lee Yan-Lam; music by James Wong Jim, Chow Gam Wing and Romeo Diaz; edited by Marco Mak Chi-sin; art directed by James Leung; photographed by Tom Lau Moon-Tong; costumes by William Chang, Bruce Yu Ka-On, Bobo Ng Bo-Ling and Chan Bo-Guen; make-up by Chi-Yeung Chan; hair: Chau Siu-Mui and Lee Lin-Dai; and sound by Chow Gam-Wing. Released July 18, 1991. 99 mins.

Joey Wong Jo-yin and Jacky Cheung Hak-yow reprised their roles (Cheung's Swordsman Yin was altered – now he's not a Taoist Master, but a money-hungry treasure seeker, happy to slaughter anybody foolish enough to steal his *geld*); Lau Siu-Ming was the Tree Demon again; but Leslie Cheung bowed out, to be replaced by Tony Leung Chiu-wai (however, Cheung does appear in the opening prologue of *A Chinese Ghost Story 3*, which reworks the climax of the first movie, with its giant tongue – tongues play a key role in *A Chinese Ghost Story 3*). Also appearing were Nina Li-chi (as Butterfly), Tiffany Lau Yuk Ting (as Jade), Cheung Yiu Sing, Hoh Choi Chow, and Lau Shun (as Reverend Bai Yun, Fong's *sifu*).

A Chinese Ghost Story 3 is a hugely enjoyable third entry in the *Chinese Ghost Story* series: it's pretty much a re-run of the story of the first movie of 1987, with two Buddhist monks taking shelter in a temple haunted by ghosts. So back come the four main characters: the hapless youth, Fong, the gorgeous ghost, Lotus, the crusty, old, Buddhist monk *sifu*, Master, and the chief villain, the Tree Demon, with Jacky Cheung playing Swordmaster Yin.[13]

The tone and attitude and atmosphere of *A Chinese Ghost Story 3* are absolutely spot-on. The cast hit exactly the right note of mock seriousness, playing the adventure straight, but leaving plenty of room for the goofy helplessness of Tony Leung's Fong, the jokey asides of Jacky Chueng's Swordsman Yin, the sweet, yearning melancholy of Joey Wong's Lotus, and some of the craziest, over-the-top performances in Hong Kong cinema – from Lau Siu-Ming as the Tree Demon and Lau Shun as the *sifu* Bai Yun.

Lau Siu-Ming's Tree Demon/ Priestess is a diva of gargantuan dimensions. By comparison with the most out-there performances of actors in the West as derranged bad guys in Western action flicks, Lau is completely excessive. Robert de Niro, Ian McKellen, Mickey Rourke, Joe Pesci, Ben Kingsley, Jeremy Irons *et al* – they are well-known for playing crazy antagonists in action cinema in the West. But, accomplished as they are, and fun to watch as they are, they are utterly eclipsed by the scorchingly high energy of Chinese performers, who start big then get bigger and bigger, where the Peking Opera traditions survive in actors who can turn their own faces into wild masks of horror, terror, ecstatic glee and truly creepy sadism.

And let's not forget Tony Leung Chiu-wai ('Little Tony Leung'), with his bald pate and wide, dark eyes: a remarkable actor (who can do anything), and one of the stalwarts of Hong Kong New Wave cinema, Leung does a fine job of stepping into Leslie Cheung's shoes (a tough act to follow – because Cheung, tho' he makes it look so easy, is a truly formidable talent). Tho' Leung doesn't quite have Cheung's incandescent star quality, Leung hits just the right note of earnestness, goofiness and cowardice; he is acting his socks off. It's a terrific comic performance which gets the balance spot-on between drama and humour (that is, for the comedy to work, *A Chinese Ghost Story 3* has to function first as a story and as a drama, and you have to buy into these characters and the situations). Known for serious roles like the gangster flicks directed by John Woo (*Bullet In the Head*, *Hard-Boiled*, etc), and later on for romantic roles (in the films of Wong Kar-wai and others), it's great to see Leung playing comedy (which he has done more than you'd think).

It's impossible not to enjoy *A Chinese Ghost Story 3* – you'd have to

---

[13] Yin makes a short speech about being trained by the older Taoist Master, to connect the two charas – altho', if this movie is meant to take place 100 years later, he would be too old (indeed, Yin says that the Master has died).

be a really miserable, really cranky and really stick-in-the-mud so-and-so not to like *A Chinese Ghost Story 3*. Seriously. Yes: this movie is going all-out to entertain *you*, the audience, and it succeeds magnificently.

The look of the 1991 *Ghost* movie is sensational, with DP Tom Lau Moon-Tong, production designer James Leung, costume designers Bruce Yu Ka-On, Bobo Ng Bo-Ling, William Chang, and Chan Bo-Guen and all the others (in make-up, practical effects, sound, editing, casting and so on) really coming up with the goods. James Wong Jim, Chow Gam Wing and Romeo Diaz compose a suitably mysterioso score for the ghostly sequences, and jaunty pop cues for the lighter scenes. (The score supports the action at every twist and turn, almost as if the musicians are playing the music live to the picture). The action choreography (by Tony Ching, Yuen Bun, Ma Yuk-shing, Cheung Yiu-sing *et al*) is of course absolutely outstanding (with cable-work creating truly awe-inspiring flying scenes, as fluid and imaginative as in any movie in film history).

Not content with staging a single performer flying on wires – across enormous distances – the stunt team hook up a host of performers on cables (and not only people, but also numerous props, including, in the finale, giant pillars of stone which erupt from the ground). And there's a new development for this film, actors are now flying in curves and circles. There is no wire-work in cinema anywhere that comes near this!

✦

A Chinese Ghost Story 3 is another love story – between a weak, effeminate man and a ravishing female ghost (the staple format of Chinese ghost stories). Turning the two humans caught up in this tale into Buddhist monks accentuates the battle between the two realms of religion and magic on one side and evil and bad karma on the other. Fong and Lotus are thrown into the middle of the battle between Bai Yun and the Tree Demon, between Buddhism and corrupt magic, between doing the right thing and doing evil. (The duels between the monks and the ghosts in *A Chinese Ghost Story 3* allow the filmmakers to indulge in evoking numerous ancient beliefs, superstitions and practices of Chinese culture and Buddhist religion: promoting such folkloric material, even if it's in a completely hokey movie-movie manner, is one of Tsui Hark's passions).[14]

Act one of *A Chinese Ghost Story 3* includes a lesbian love scene – well, a scene that skirts very close to lesbian erotica without delving into Category III (porn) territory. In a scene that might've come out of *Green Snake,* Lotus and Butterfly are first introduced in *A Chinese Ghost Story 3* in a close embrace in their chambers (where all is pieces of floaty, coloured cloth), sharing what seems to be smoke from an opium pipe. It's girls together in a teasing, intimate set-up that's a recurring motif in Tsui Hark's cinema (drugs, beautiful girls, sex, and even tattoos are laid out in a voluptuous scene lit and photographed by DP Tom Lau Moon-tong like a Chinese painting. As usual in a Tony Ching film, every single scene has wind machines billowing the hair and costumes).

---

[14] The talisman in the 1991 *Ghost* movie is a golden statue of the Buddha (which performs many duties, not least reminding Fong of his spiritual calling as a Buddhist monk). The monks are transporting the precious Buddha statue, and of course the hapless Fong loses it.

The lesbian scene leads directly on to the let's-show-how-nasty-the-villains-are sequence, where the Tree Demon presides over a decadent court of ghosts who slay a band of ruffians. The centrepiece is, of all things, a pool (a more extravagant version of the wooden baths of the previous *Chinese Ghost Stories*). Lotus and Butterfly play the sirens that lure the men into their deadly domain, from which there is no escape. Out flicks the Tree Demon's tongue (in a remarkable monster p.o.v. shot, across the surface of the water), and into the gullet of its first victim. (And in a nifty piece of screenwriting, the brigands sneaked into this area in the first place because they caught a glimpse of the golden Buddha that the two monks were carrying in a restaurant; even cleverer, it's Swordsman Yin who accidentally slices open the cloth hiding the statue).

The lure of gold in *A Chinese Ghost Story 3* brings in once again the issue of money in a Hong Kong picture, that hyper-capitalist city of, as Chinese movies have it, gamblers, gangsters, hookers and hustlers (there are two treasure-seeking groups in *A Chinese Ghost Story 3*).

Yes – this's how Swordsman Yin is introduced in the first reel of *A Chinese Ghost Story 3* (in the opening sequence) – cutting up the thieves who've stolen his money: it's the replay of the sheltering-from-a-storm scene in the first *Ghost* film, where the hapless scholar found himself in the midst of a bitter feud. Comedy is uppermost, tho', as poor Fong has blood sprayed over him repeatedly and – in a classic, Tsui Harkian joke – body parts too (and afterwards, he's told to bury the corpses by his *sifu* who, in a great gag, just happens to have a little hoe in his robes!).

✦

Love – and sex... *A Chinese Ghost Story 3* squeezes an entire second act out of Joey Wong's spirit Lotus trying to seduce Tony Leung's monk Fong. That's all it is, for 20 or 30 minutes: a man, a woman... one wants it, one doesn't want it... the movie happily trots out the old narrative chestnuts of a beautiful, willing woman and an unwilling (but handsome) man (that it's two famous and attractive stars of the early Nineties period, Wong and Leung, enhances the sequence no end – Leung was something of a pin-up at the time, too).

And the first act of *Ghost 3* had already delivered that scenario between Lotus and Fong – intercut with scenes of Bai Yun trying to draw out the ghosts using his Buddhist magic (Bai Yun has to be taken away from the scene, so that Lotus can go to work on Fong). Lotus attempts many times to seduce Fong, resulting in all sorts of amazingly dynamic physical acting: this is the polar opposite of a romantic comedy where two people stand and spout clever-clever quips that a team of writers have spent months re-writing. Instead of Western cinema's continual and dogged insistence on dialogue-heavy romantic comedies, and the static blocking of two actors just standing there, the Chinese action approach, steeped in Peking Opera performance styles, is gloriously kinetic and inventive.

In their first encounter, Lotus flutters into the Orchid Temple when Fong foolishly opens the front door, and wafts about in distress, crying about ghosts like a scared child. Joey Wong captures the mock fear and sneaky seduction of Lotus as she dances around Fong, trips, falls, and pulls him on top of her (repeatedly). The Peking Opera approach puts bodies in continual motion, striking amazing poses – all across the floor, and other parts of the set.

This is the Hong Kong film equivalent of a seduction scene in a Hollywood musical – musical cinema (and musical theatre) is really the closest equivalent to something like this, where movement, rhythm, timing, music, lighting, costumes, and practical effects work together to form a dazzling combination that evokes romance, beauty, comedy, and danger.

This is mesmerizing cinema, where each shot is conceived as if starting from scratch, as if each shot stands alone, as if each shot could be The One, as if each shot has the potential to become the Greatest Shot Ever Filmed.

Indeed, this is how Hong Kong cinema films action: instead of filming all of the shots from one side (from one actor's point-of-view), then adjusting everything (lights included), to film from the other side, which is the Western/ Hollywood way, Hong Kong cinema films each shot and each piece of action individually.

But the shots *are* conceived as part of a sequence, with a flow, a rhythm, a timing. Hong Kong action cinema is more compelling than many other forms of action cinema perhaps because it constructs its action sequences in this manner. The camerawork and the editing follow the rhythm, tempo and the flow of the movement as it was filmed on the set, rather than a pre-conceived series of storyboards, for example, or sticking to a rigid shot-counter-shot pattern, or filming tons of footage and hoping it will will cut together.

So now in the second act of *A Chinese Ghost Story 3* the silly-but-fun device of the extra-long tongue that the villain deployed so memorably in the previous *A Chinese Ghost Story* movies (and seen in the prologue of this movie), becomes a motif in the seduction scene, as Lotus French kisses Fong. And French kisses him again (to get out some snake venom, she claims; snakes are everywhere in this movie. And there's the business of the lost Buddha statue (which is then found to be broken), which also adds to the comedy in act 2).

Really, all we we're watching is a couple of actors goofing around on a lavish temple set (with occasional appearances from a third actor, Lau Shun), but it's amusing, it's entertaining, it's fun. Sure, it's very conventional romance-plus-comedy, and this time not even a fervently radical film critic could link this humorous, romantic sequence to the 1997 Hand-over in Hong Kong! (Tho' that wouldn't stop them trying! There are some critics who see *every* movie made between 1982 and 1997 in Hong Kong as relating in some form or other to the 1997 Hand-over!).

But *A Chinese Ghost Story 3* is very clearly designed mainly as a piece of entertainment in which the local, Cantonese audience can *forget* about all of that, and simply watch a pantomime about ghosts and monks and demons (it's a high-class panto delivered by a team of *very* talented veterans).

A Chinese Ghost Story 3 has an impressive scope and size, with its village sets and hills, fields and forests, its temples and palaces, yet much of the film comprises only three actors: Tony Leung, Joey Wong and Lau Shun. But they are so good, you don't notice for a moment that whole scenes and then whole sections of the film slip by which feature only two actors on a single set (such as the Orchid Temple at night).

✦

Act two of *A Chinese Ghost Story 3* climaxes, as expected, with a Big Action Sequence: the re-appearance of the Tree Demon, and an absolutely remarkable magical duel between the Tree Demon and Master Bai Yun – the combination of practical effects and optical effects is as inventive as any in fantasy cinema. The imagery of the Buddhist *sifu* balancing on his staff and the Tree Demon conjuring a battery of elemental forces to kill him are incredible – water effects, fire, explosions, etc (the film uses one of Tony Ching's signature images – a wall of water exploding upwards behind a sorcerous figure, also seen in the *Swordsman* series). The feeling for texture and atmosphere is so acute, you can feel the elements of fire and water as they interact with the characters. (No need for movie enhancements like I.M.A.X., or 3-D, or flight simulator platforms, or smell-o-rama, when you've got movie-making this sensuous).

Meanwhile, the more comical and romantic aspects of the battles between humans and ghosts occur in the scenes between Fong and Lotus, as a counterpart of the epic Bai Yun versus Tree Demon scenes: here's Fong hurrying about, torn between helping his Master and feeling sorry for Lotus.

The magical staff (a *khakkhara*, also known as a Zen stick and pewter staff) that Bai Yun carries is exploited inventively here – the monk throws it at Lotus, pinning her painfully to the wall of the Orchid Temple. Bai Yun calls for help from Fong, and Fong, having freed Lotus from the staff, takes him the staff. The act two climax includes numerous bits of intricate, physical business that play out very rapidly. But all of the action – and the comedy – is still fixed firmly to the fundamental characterizations of the four principal players (the two monks and the two spirits).

As Tsui Hark has explained many times, action comes with a story, and a style, and a look – it's not merely action for action's sake. Thus, the wild and over-the-top action sequences in a movie such as *A Chinese Ghost Story 3* are always rooted in the narrative context, in the characterizations, in their relationships, their conflicts, their goals and their motivations.

✦

Many, many elements in *A Chinese Ghost Story 3* are pure Tsui Hark: the scene where money-grubbing Swordsman Yin finds his coins on the ground talking back to him and scooting into a nearby pool to disappear (as charmed by Bai Yun) is pure Tsui (and pure Walt Disney). Animated in stopmotion, the coins talk back to their owner (and they also bow to prove they belong to him). Money is such an important motif in Hong Kong cinema, it's no surprise that Tsui would eventually include animated, talking coins.

Another very Tsui Harkian sequence is the crowded village scene, where everybody it seems is a sword-maker or a sword-seller (including some swords with ridiculous designs, like a convention of fantasy cosplayers and their homemade weaponry). Tsui also loves scenes where whole crowds act as one, in a humorous fashion – doing a double take altogether, for instance.

The rivalry between the two female ghosts (Joey Wong's Lotus and Nina Li Chi's Butterfly) is another Tsui Harkian ingredient in *A Chinese Ghost Story 3*. The twitching of Bai Yun's over-large ears is another Tsui-ism[15] (later, they grow and cover his eyes, when the Tree Demon captures him).

The floppy ears bit of business occurs at the close of the act two finale – really, it's a rather artificial way of delaying the final smackdown between the heroes and the villains: Bai Yun tells his pupil to hurry into town to have the golden Buddha statue fixed (it's needed to defeat the Tree Demon).

◆

So the golden Buddha statue MacGuffin is still doing some narrative work in act three of *A Chinese Ghost Story 3* – Fong heads into town to get it repaired, only to have the blacksmiths and ruffians get the better of him (there was a hint of that when they spurned Bai Yun begging for food[16]). It's here that Fong bumps into Swordsman Yin, which re-introduces Yin into the proceedings, in time for the finale. (Yin saves Bai Yun from the thugs, but for a price. He constantly calculates his fee on his abacus, while knowing that Bai Yun is penniless like him. Yin agrees to help Bai Yun rescue his Master with the promise of remuneration).

In act three of the second *Chinese Ghost Story* sequel, the French romantic farce elements are re-introduced, involving Fong and Lotus with the added complications of greedy Swordsman Yin, and the catty, resentful sister of Lotus, Butterfly (this occurs just before the action section of the finale). The many jokes include the worldly Yin, who doesn't have a problem fooling around with women, having to watch the supposedly chaste monk Fong being kissed into submission by Lotus. It's just not fair! (The humour is enhanced by the casting of pop star Jacky Cheung as Yin – a singer who's used to the adulation of girls).

Two guys, and two girls: the sequence is played like French farce and screwball comedy: very fast, and very silly. Lotus hurls herself at Bai Yun, after Butterfly has also burst into the temple to do the same. Swordsman Yin watches in disbelief as not one but two beautiful women throw themselves at Bai Yun's feet (in frustration, he performs a sword dance, this movie's version of the dance of the Taoist Master in the first film.

---

[15] 'Tsui Hark's ability to make something incredible and outlandish out of ordinary facial features such as eyes, ears and tongue must mark him as a unique filmmaker', remarked Stephen Teo (1997, 229).
[16] Food is another Tsui-ian motif in *A Chinese Ghost Story 3* – Fong is perpetually hungry. His Master talks about prayers and the spiritual life, but Fong can't exist on words alone.

Unusually, *A Chinese Ghost Story 3* doesn't have Jacky Cheung sing).

There's a raid on the Tree Demon's digs by Fong and Swordsman Yin, where they dash in and out rapidly, with the action as swift as a manic kids' cartoon (but with the rescue of Bai Yun put off for the finale). The stunt crew somehow depict *sifu* Bai Yun and Lotus zipping across the ground. Butterfly and Lotus are prominent here, and there's a third sister, Jade (Tiffany Lau Yuk Ting), who unfortunately gets in the way of the bitchy rivalry between Lotus and Butterfly. And the Tree Demon has his arm cut off (by Swordsman Yin) – but it grows back again.

✦

To climax the 1991 *Ghost* installment, and all three *Chinese Ghost Story* movies, Tony Ching Siu-tung, Tsui Hark and the team conjure up a truly remarkable barrage of action sequences which assault the audience like World War Three. As with the previous two *Chinese Ghost Story* flicks, the finale is an enormous battle between the good guys (the two monks and the Swordsman) and the villains (the Tree Demon, plus the Mountain Devil, Butterfly, and their henchmen) – with Lotus as the wild card caught in the middle of the crossfire.

The action sequences in the finale of *A Chinese Ghost Story 3* are simply insane,[17] with nothing in Western cinema coming anywhere near them. By the time of this third movie, the filmmaking team had achieved a sophistication of visual effects cinema which blows everyone else out of the water.

There's so much enjoy in the climax of *A Chinese Ghost Story 3* – how about, for starters, the scene where the heroes fly on a magic carpet (made from the *sifu*'s cloak) in between stone pillars smashing upwards thru the ground? How about the insanely hysterical performance by Lau Siu-Ming as the Tree Demon, battling the heroes while poor Fong is strung up in the air with red ropes?[18] How about the Tree Demon impersonating Lotus at the night festival (so you get two Joey Wongs running in slow motion)? How about the Tree Demon's demise in an extraordinary full-body burn scene? How about the conception of the Mountain Demon as a grimacing head of dirt and dust, and a walking temple with arms? How about Fong being turned by his *sifu* into a man-sized, golden Buddha and flying high above the clouds to greet the sunrise and reflect the spiritual light down into the underworld built by the Mountain Devil, to dissolve the monster in a series of incredible explosions? How about the beautiful, vibrant orange colours and shafts of light to depict the sun bursting into the netherworld?

Tsui Hark inserts his beloved Lion Dancing into *A Chinese Ghost Story 3*, as he did in every historical movie he produced in this period. In a scene of flaming torches and a boisterous crowd, Lion Dancers perform: only after the movie shifts back to the Orchid Temple at night is it revealed that our heroes have never escaped: they've been caught in an illusion of the Tree Demon.

---
17 The finale of *A Chinese Ghost Story 3* employs every trick cinema has ever developed, and invents some of its own, too.
18 And Butterfly trying to seduce him – Fong is fated to have beautiful women throwing themselves at him in *A Chinese Ghost Story 3*.

The welter of visual effects stomp across the finale like the Imperial Army: as soon as the giant tongue of the Tree Demon has been attacked with flying swords and bombs by the heroes, and the Tree Demon burns to death, the second villain erupts from Hell: the Mountain Devil. The sequence is a variation on the finales of both of the previous *Chinese Ghost Story* pictures, this time with a temple coming to life to stalk the heroes, who're fleeing on a magic carpet.

It sounds amazing, and it is: the combination of models, puppeteering, animatronics, and astonishing practical effects (pyrotechnics, smoke, dust, fire) is spellbinding. Whole segments of the sets are puppeteered using wires to create wild images of devastation, of crumbling stone pillars, of billowing dirt from explosions.

Even with the film sped up, the action directors (Ching, Ma, Yuen, and Cheung) conjure up remarkable stuntwork – performers are sent flying into every corner of the sets and the frame; actors slide across the ground at 50 m.p.h.; Lotus grabs Bai Yun and dives into the ground.

The pell-mell approach resembles a quickfire comedy with one gag hot on the heels of the one on the screen. This movie simply does not acknowledge that something *can't* be done, that conventional physics would not allow the human body to travel that fast, or to bend like that. No one says 'no' to Tony Ching!

Anything seems possible here, as cinema is re-invented in scenes of breathtaking imagination. Often it's the miracle of *editing* that is making it all work: Tony Ching, Tsui Hark and editor Marco Mak Chi-sin possess a feeling for how images cut together as skilful as anyone in the history of cinema or television.

4

A CHINESE GHOST STORY: THE TSUI HARK ANIMATION

Siu Sin

A Chinese Ghost Story: The Tsui Hark Animation[19] (1997, *Siu Sin* in Cantonese; *Xiaoqian* in Mandarin), was the first feature overseen by Tsui Hark in animation – a dream of his, probably, of many decades (ever since he started making movies in his early teens).

The voice cast of *A Chinese Ghost Story: The Tsui Hark Animation* is a bunch of Tsui Hark regulars: Nicky Wu, Charlie Yeung, Anita Yuen, Raymond Wong, Eric Kot, James Wong Jim, Sylvia Chang and Kelly Chen (all the usual suspects – 'my friends, performers and stars'), with Tsui voicing the dog, Solid Gold. Writer: Tsui Hark. Produced by Triangle Staff/ Film Workshop. Dis. by Golden Harvest. Directors: Andrew Chen Jun-man and Tetsuya Endo. Producers: Nansun Shi Nan-sheng, Tsuneo Leo-sato, Charles Heung and Meileen Choo. Music: Ricky Ho and James Wong Jim. Animation director: Tetsuya Endo. Character designers: Frankie Chung and Takashi Nakamura. Editor: Chi-sin Tsui Kak. The budget was U.S. $7 million. Released July 31, 1997. 84 mins.

If *A Chinese Ghost Story: The Tsui Hark Animation* looks like a Japanese *animé*, that's because it is: the animation was produced by Triangle Staff in Japan, an *animé* house whose credits include *Macross Plus, Serial Experiments Lain, Space Pirate Mito, Catnapped, Ultra Nyan* and *Hyper Doll*. One of the animation directors was the remarkable Takashi Nakamura (b. 1955, Yamanashi Prefecture), the chief animator on *Akira* (for many the greatest animation ever), with credits including: *Robot Carnival, Fantastic Children, Peter Pan, Nausicaä of the Valley of the Wind,* and he directed *Catnapped* and *Tree of Palme*.

Triangle Staff worked with Film Workshop to produce the movie, so *A Chinese Ghost Story: The Tsui Hark Animation* is a kind of Chinese-Japanese hybrid, tho' the style and the approach is very Japanese; while

---
[19] The subtitle, 'The Tsui Hark Animation', has a mogul's air about it – as if Tsui was now of the stature of Alfred Hitchcock or Steven Spielberg (well, for some, he was – and he is).

the subject – Chinese supernatural tales, is distinctly Chinese.[20] But anyone who's seen any *animé* will know that Japanese cartoons are full of this kind of fantasy and adventure, and Chinese mythologies have popped up in Japanese animation many times.

Thus, the influence of Hayao Miyazaki is easy to spot. Walt Disney is in there, too, of course[21] (the first animation that Tsui Hark – and many of us – encountered was Disney), as well as more recent Western animations. The ghost town has distinctly Tim Burtonian influences (including *The Nightmare Before Christmas,* 1993).

Tsui Hark expressed disappointment with the animation in *A Chinese Ghost Story*, the use of 3-D,[22] the variations in the quality in the animation, and with the production set-up. Tsui discovered that animation requires a different kind of organization from live-action: it's a discipline that demands an enormous amount of work which has to be sustained over months and months (setting up an animation production team and pipeline from scratch for a feature film is a massive undertaking. The animation business, too, is *very* different from the live-action business). It appears that there were disagreements about the look and the approach of *A Chinese Ghost Story: The Tsui Hark Animation*; Tsui complained that the traditional animators in Japan didn't want to work with the Chinese designs (LM, 129).

However, there's no doubt that some of the production crew in Japan were veterans of animation, whereas Tsui Hark, despite his enormous experience in filmmaking (including animation added to live-action plates), probably had less experience of *animé*.

◆

A Chinese Ghost Story: The Tsui Hark Animation is a fun, fast-paced and colourful version of the Pu Songling stories and the three *Chinese Ghost Story* movies. There's plenty of action, plenty of goofy humour, some wistful romance, and of course spectacle. There are songs, too (mostly by James Wong Jim, who also plays Red Beard).

And there's no doubt that *A Chinese Ghost Story: The Tsui Hark Animation* is another of Tsui Hark's pæans to the riches of Chinese history and tradition.

It's got the superpower battles between Buddhist monks flying around the sky, it's got the hapless tax collector caught in the midst of this out-size, supernatural world (now aided by a classic dog sidekick), and a ghost town. The Reincarnation Train is a fun concept – a flying train that clearly draws on the famous Cat-bus[23] in *My Neighbor Totoro* (Hayao Miyazaki, 1988), though in the form of a Chinese dragon.

The ironic commentary in *A Chinese Ghost Story: The Tsui Hark*

---

[20] The animated *Chinese Ghost Story* is 'as much a reworking of *Zu* as any of the *Chinese Ghost Story* films' (Lisa Morton, 127).
[21] *A Chinese Ghost Story: The Tsui Hark Animation* was 'a deliberate attempt to make a cross between Japanese *animé* and American Disney', Tsui Hark said in 1998.
[22] The 3-D technology was still in its infancy in 1997, and there were problems with it.
[23] The Cat-bus – the *nekobasu* – is one of Hayao Miyazaki's original and most memorable creations, a giant, stripey ginger cat, with eyes as headlights, and mice eyes illuminating the front and rear. As a magical transport, the Cat-bus is a perfect creation: it looks like it has always existed, like the best artworks. There must have always been a Cat-bus, surely? The Knight-Bus in the *Harry Potter* books seems to have drawn on the Cat-bus.

Animation on Chinese myths and movies about Chinese myths is amusing – and of course, Tsui Hark was more responsible for the recent spate of Chinese fable/ fantasy movies than most individuals on the planet.

The characters were aged down – to early teens, to match the target audience, perhaps. Which inevitably scuppers the intensity and operatic tragedy of the romance of the 1987-1990-1991 *Chinese Ghost Story* movies (that was Tsui Hark's decision – to make it funnier, to have 'a totally cute version of the story' (LM, 130), to have early teens expressing emotions more suited to late teens). And at the end, an amusing sequence has all of the characters regressing to babyhood.

The 1997 cartoon, of course, lacks the two superpowers of the live-action movies – the actors Leslie Cheung Kwok-wing and Joey Wong Cho-yin. (The character animation of Ning Choi-san can't compete with an actor as incredible as Leslie Cheung. Indeed, most of the time in *A Chinese Ghost Story: The Tsui Hark Animation,* Ning is gawping in awe or fear, or he's yelling, 'Siu Shin!!').[24]

But *A Chinese Ghost Story: The Tsui Hark Animation* is very romantic, with romance as a key element: Ning Choi-san has been jilted by his girlfriend, Lan, and in the first act dreams of her, remembers her, and encounters another beauty, Shine (in a procession in the ghost town). So women as aloof, beautiful and frustratingly unattainable figures are one of the motifs of *A Chinese Ghost Story: The Tsui Hark Animation.* It all ends happily, of course – Ning is re-united with his beloved Shine, as humans, on Earth.

On the down side, *A Chinese Ghost Story: The Tsui Hark Animation* is marred with too many action scenes looking and sounding the same – this is an issue of tone and of the script, which Tsui Hark, as co-writer and co-producer, might've addressed.

The characters zooming thru the air recall *Zu: Warriors From the Magic Mountain* (the re-make of *Zu* would use digital animation to send its characters flying around the sky). Maybe it works for a ten year-old audience, but there's a lack of weight and substance to the animation and the action (precisely what Tsui Hark complained about in regard to *Star Wars: The Phantom Menace,* a couple of years later – and the 2001 *Legend of Zu* was Tsui's reply to *The Phantom Menace*).

---

[24] To be fair, Leslie Cheung also spends quite a bit of time shouting, 'Siu-shin!!'

A Chinese Ghost Story 2 (1990), this page and over.

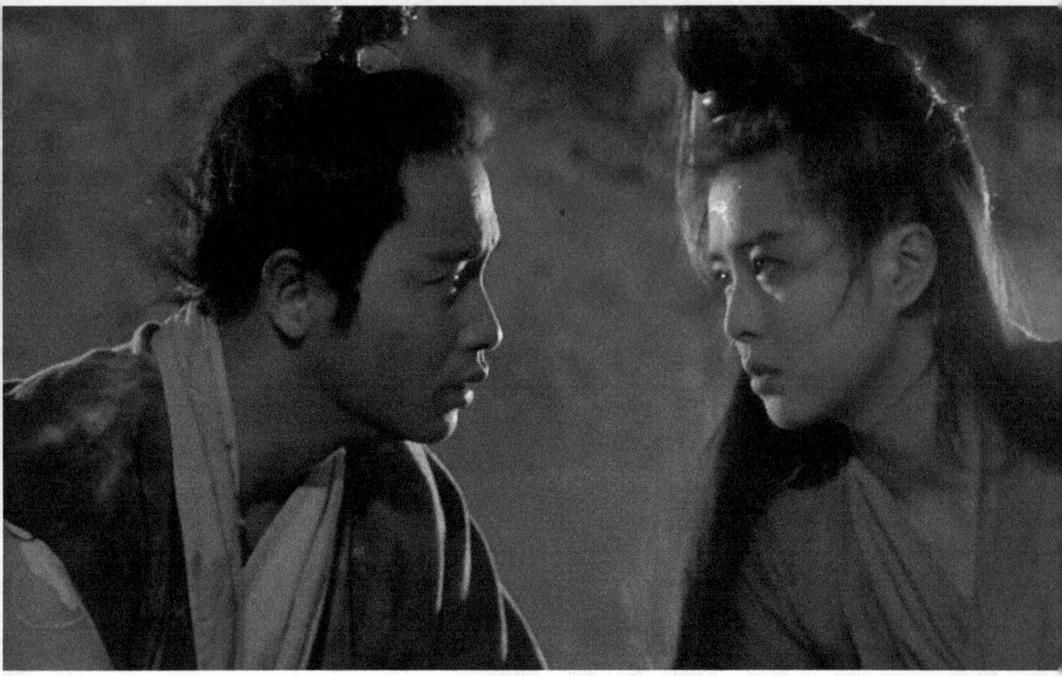

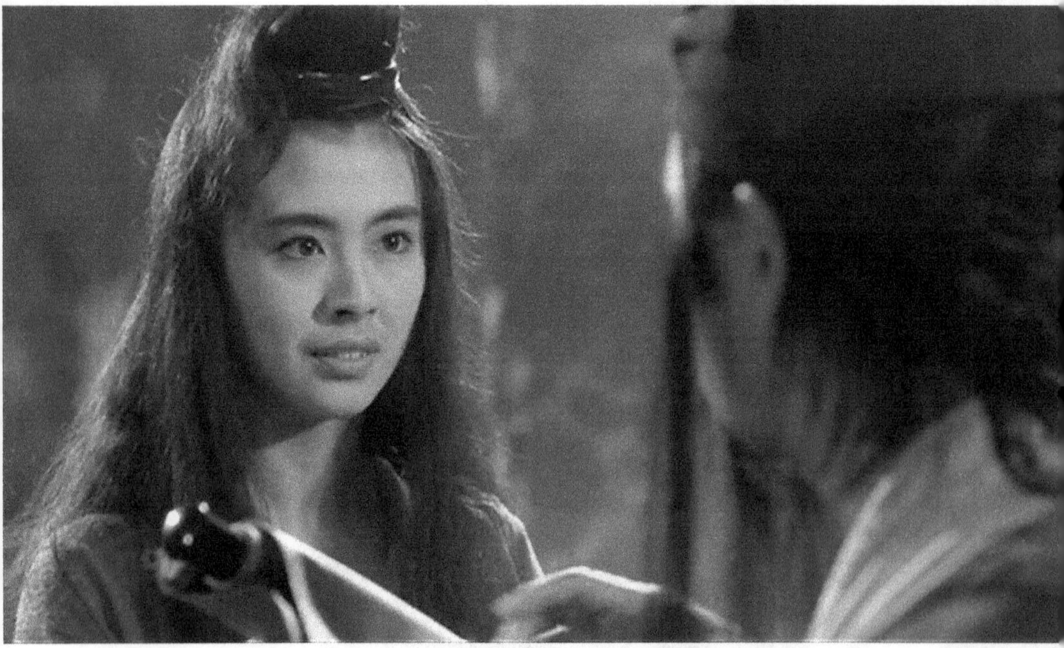

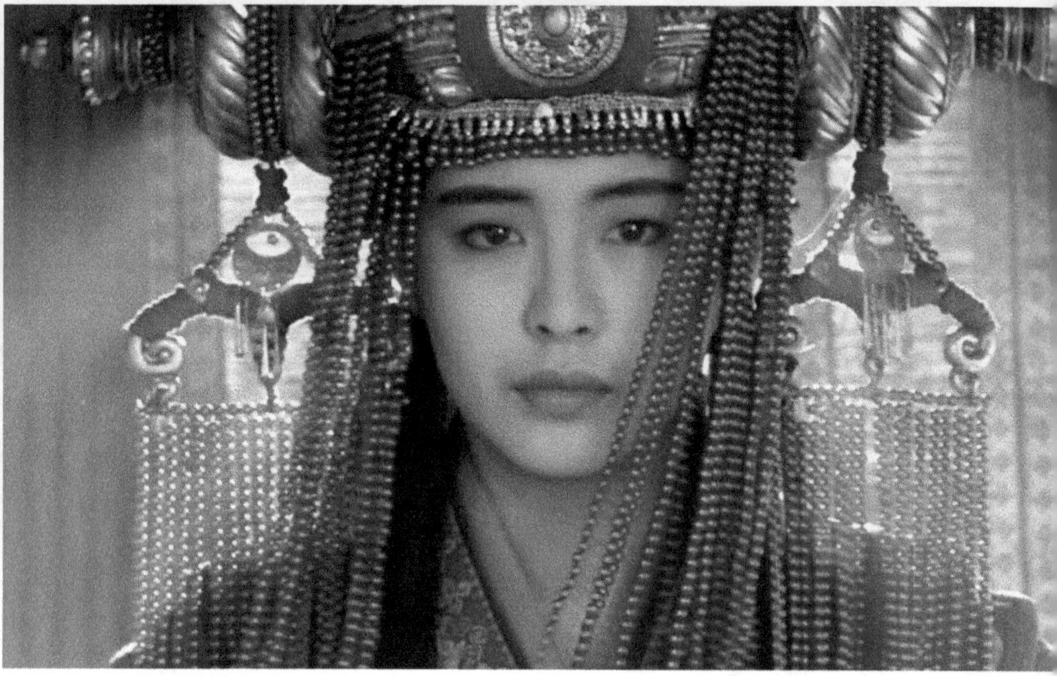

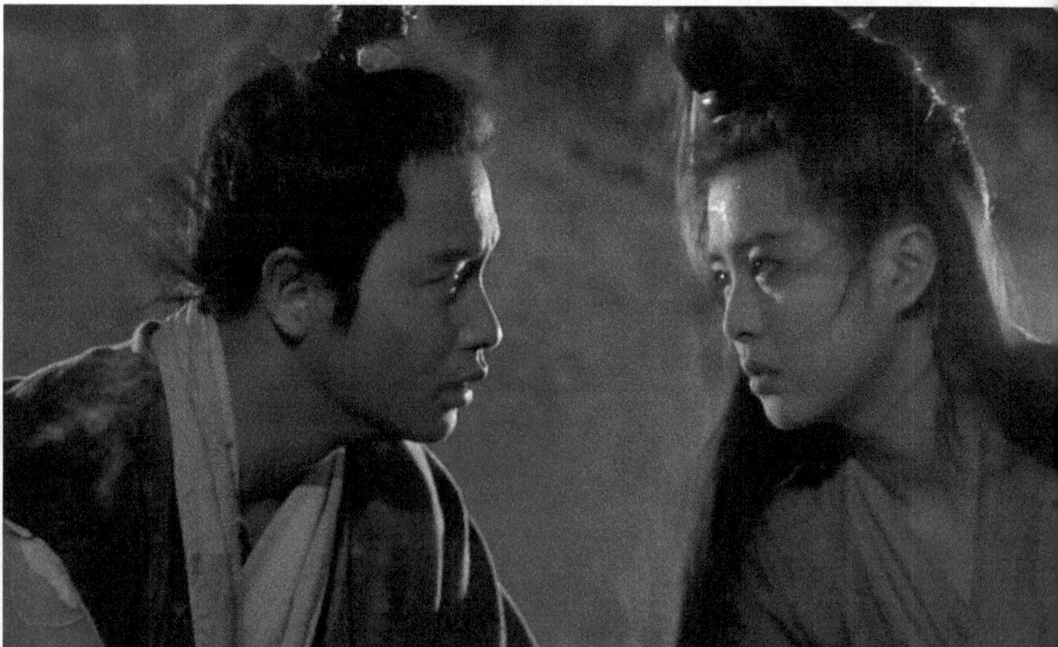

A Chinese Ghost Story 3 (1991), this page and over.

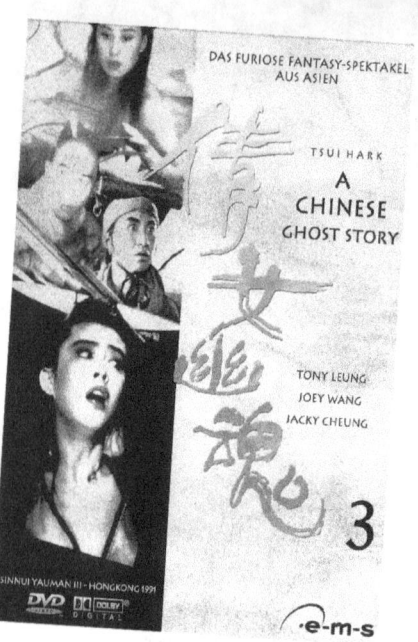

愛は魔王に勝てるか。

利智　梁朝偉　王祖賢　午馬　張學友　劉兆銘
小蝶　十方　小卓　　　　燕赤霞　姥姥

A Chinese Ghost Story (1997).

5

MOVIES RELATED TO
A CHINESE GHOST STORY

THE ENCHANTING SHADOW

A Chinese Ghost Story (1987) is in part a remake of *The Enchanting Shadow* (*Qian Yu Youhun*, 1960), an important Hong Kong movie which was entered in the Cannes Film Festival and also for the Academy Awards. Made at Shaws, *The Enchanting Shadow* was produced by Run Run Shaw and Duwen Zhou, wr. by Wang Yueting from Pu Songling's book, dir. by Li Han-hsiang, and starred Zhao Lei, Betty Loh Ti, Yang Chih-ching, Tang Ruoqing, and Lee Kwan. Released: Aug 17, 1960. 83 mins.

    The Enchanting Shadow followed the adventures of Ning Caichen (Zhao Lei) in an abandoned temple, where he encounters the Taoist priest Yang Chixia (Yang Chi-ching), and the ghost Nie Xiaqian (Betty Loh Ti).

    The Enchanting Shadow is an atmospheric Shaw Brothers production, filmed largely in the studio (like *A Chinese Ghost Story*, and most horror movies). It's illuminating to compare the cinematic approaches of the two films to the same material from Pu Songling: the 1960 Shaws movie is stagey and static by comparison with the rapidfire, kinetic approach of the 1987 Cinema City/ Film Workshop version. The 1960 film relies a good deal on dialogue to carry the story, while the 1987 film embraces action and martial arts.

    When you compare the two versions of a Chinese legend, you can see how Tsui Hark and company approach many of their remakes: they add action, martial arts, swordplay, comedy, eroticism, sleaze, visual effects and gore. They resort to the gestures of exploitation cinema for the horror, for example, while mixing it with a knowing, ironic sense of humour (*A Chinese Ghost Story* plays to its audience, aware of how ciné-literate they are).

    The 1987 movie eroticizes the 1960 version considerably – now the ghost has sex with her victims, before stepping aside for her monstrous mistress. *A Chinese Ghost Story* teases the viewer with partial nudity, too. *The Enchanted Shadow* moves away from depicting the gore and threat of the attacks: instead, there's an off-screen scream, and the characters hurry over to see what's happened. The shot of the feet of the victims oozing blood evokes the vampirism. Meanwhile, *A Chinese Ghost Story* dives head-first into portraying the gore and the horror.

Action is everywhere in the 1987 remake, adding swordplay a-plenty and martial arts. The action sequences expand greatly on those in *The Enchanting Shadow*. Individual scenes are shorter, and the cutting is inevitably more rapid. With Tsui Hark producing and Tony Ching directing, the 1987 remake is heavy on visual effects and cinematic trickery. If there's a gimmick they haven't tried before, they'll use it here. The 1960 movie is rich in atmosphere, but the 1987 version adds plenty of practical effects such as textures (such as smoke, fire, rain, etc).

With so many additions and reworkings of the original film of 1960, *A Chinese Ghost Story* is pretty much a different movie. It employs the narrative framework of the 1960 Shaws version, but it's a considerable departure from a straight remake.

One of Tsui Hark's approaches to remakes is bring something new to the original, and this certainly occurs with *A Chinese Ghost Story*'s attitude towards *The Enchanting Shadow*.

PORTRAIT OF A NYMPH

Several movies, as usual in the Hong Kong entertainment industry, cashed in on the success of *A Chinese Ghost Story* in 1987. One of the better ones was *Portrait of a Nymph* (a.k.a. *Picture of a Nymph*, 1988), which included some of the same cast as *A Chinese Ghost Story* (Joey Wong, Lam Wai and Wu Ma, who also directed). Also appearing were: Yuen Biao, Lawrence Ng, Sit Chi-lun, Yuen Wah, Yip So, and Elizabeth Lee Mei-fung.

Portrait of a Nymph was wr. by Chan Ka-Cheong and Wu Ma, produced by Sammo Hung, music by James Wong Jim, Romeo Diaz and Sherman Chow Gam-Cheung, DPs: Abdul M. Rumjahn, Tom Lau Moon-Tong and Raymond Lam Fai-Tai, costumes by Bobo Ng Bo-Ling, Kenneth Yee Chung-Man and Siu Wing-Yee, art dir. by Ng Bo-Jan and Kenneth Yee Chung-Man, with action dir. by Hung (some of the team also worked on *A Chinese Ghost Story* – composers Diaz and Wong, DP Tom Lau, art. dir. Yee Chung-Man, etc). Released Mch 18, 1988, 95 mins.

Portrait of a Nymph featured many of the same elements as *A Chinese Ghost Story* – the mediæval setting, the young, male character, the ethereal woman, fantasy and the supernatural, swordplay and magical combat, waterside scenes, smoky,[1] blue nights, etc. *Portrait of a Nymph* cast two young, male leads, though, splitting the hero into two (played by

---

[1] Way too much smoke – in some scenes, the practical effects team smother everything in smoke.

Biao and Ng. As the hapless scholar, Ng, who often played similar roles (such as in the *Sex and Zen* films), is charming and effective, but he's no Leslie Cheung. Ah, but who is? Cheung is a unique and very special star).

Portrait of a Nymph employs the MacGuffin of *A Chinese Ghost Story* in a novel way: it has Joey Wong's ghost living inside the portrait of herself. In the finale, our heroes also dive through the painting into a spectral world.

Portrait of a Nymph makes great use of sets suggested by minimal means. For ex, in the ghost-world, beyond the painting, the throne room is merely a mass of white sheets and banners, hanging every which way across the screen. With some clever backlighting by one of the cinematographers (Abdul M. Rumjahn, Tom Lau Moon-Tong or Raymond Lam Fai-Tai), and their lighting gaffers (Wong Chi-Ming and Wong Pak-Wing), all of those white cloths become a lavish setting.

With some of the 'Seven Little Fortunes' on the team, and with Sammo Hung and his stunt team choreographing business, the action in *Portrait of a Nymph* was bound to be impressive. An early fight pits Yuen Wah against Yuen Biao, with Wah as one of those wizards with magical eyebrows that expand into weapons (like Sammo's character Whitebrows in *Zu: Warriors From the Magic Mountain*). *Portrait of a Nymph* makes the most of Biao's famous acrobatic skills (he is somersaulting and leaping all over the sets).

Altho' Sammo Hung is known for his grounded action choreography – where actors or stunt people perform actions which a human could do, he has of course directed sequences filled with wires, as here in *Portrait of a Nymph.* This is a romantic fantasy piece, where the rules of 'reality' are jettisoned: Joey Wong as a ghost, for instance, can't trudge across the set like a regular person – she has to swoop and soar. And Yuen Biao's acrobatic warrior needs to fly, too, if he's going to keep up with airborne spirits.

The finale has the charas flying about everywhere – and there's an innovative use of palanquins, one of the staples of the Chinese, historical film genre. So Wu Ma is soaring around in a red palanquin where he's beset by a phalanx of other palanquins. It's a wonderfully silly and very over-the-top sequence (we know that this movie is going to end with some out-there action. That is absolutely mandatory in a movie like this).

Portrait of a Nymph doesn't achieve the same miraculous blend of comedy, romance, drama and horror of *A Chinese Ghost Story* (but few films do). It's funny, it's romantic, it's thrilling in sections, but it doesn't soar like *A Chinese Ghost Story*. Joey Wong swans about in exactly the same manner as Nip Siu-shin the ghost in *A Chinese Ghost Story*, and Lawrence Ng is charmingly luckless, a bit useless but earnest, but *Portrait of a Nymph* certainly doesn't possess the grand passion of *A Chinese Ghost Story*. Even tho' *A Chinese Ghost Story* was a fantasy comedy, it exhibited a genuine substance and pathos too, resulting in one of the most poignant endings in all of Chinese cinema.

A CHINESE GHOST STORY (2011)

Several films produced/ directed by Tsui Hark have been re-made, and Tsui has of course been involved with many remakes himself (including updating his own movies as director). Tony Ching, too, has worked on many remakes, and in 2011 he was remaking the 1993 Tsui Hark movie *Green Snake* (as *The Sorcerer and the White Snake*).

The remake of *A Chinese Ghost Story* (a.k.a. *A Chinese Fairy Tale*, Mandarin: *Qiàn Nu You Hún*) was produced in 2011 by Golden Sun Films, prod. by Lai Jun-kei, Peng Yi and Xu Jianhai, wr. by Charcoal Tan Cheung, dir. by Wilson Yip Wai-Shun, DP: Arthur Wong, art dir. by Jeff Mak Gwok-Keung, editors: Tang Man-To and Cheung Ka-Fai, costumes by Bobo Ng Bo-Ling, music by Ronald Ng Luk-Sing, and action dirs. were Alan Chui Chung-San, Fan Chin-Hung and Ma Yuk-sing. It starred Louis Koo (as Swordsman Yin), Liu Yifei (as Nip Siu-shin), Yu Shaoqun (as Ning Choi-san), Kara Hui, Elvis Tsui and Wang Danyi-li. Released Apl 22, 2011. 100 mins.

✦

The 2011 remake was dedicated to Leslie Cheung, and used his theme song from the 1987 movie.[2] (It's a curious way of offering a tribute – a giant concert might be better, or a tribute documentary, with the proceeds going to a charity which helps with the psychological issues that Cheung suffered from).

Some of the cast of the 2011 *Ghost* remake appeared in the original *Chinese Ghost Story* films (such as Elvis Tsui), and Charcoal Tan Cheung was one of Tsui Hark's regular writers (of *New Dragon Gate Inn*, for example, which Tony Ching choreographed, and *The Swordsman 3*, which Ching directed).

The 2011 movie recalls several North American movies of a similar kind, such as *Van Helsing* (2004), the *Underworld* series (2003 onwards), and of course many recent superhero flicks. Some critics reckoned the producers had the *Twilight* franchise in their sights, in terms of appealing to a young audience.

✦

So, *A Chinese Ghost Story* in 2011 turned out to be a prestige update of the Tony Ching-Tsui Hark masterpiece (my view of remakes is: remake anything, but leave much-loved films or important films or masterpieces alone). A handsome-looking production[3] with a strong cast, *A Chinese Ghost Story* was filled with digital visual effects, just as the 1987 movie had been a visual effects feast. (Of course, there are practical, in-front-of-the-camera effects everywhere in the 2011 version, too, as there are in any movie which uses digital or computer-assisted work. Why? Because live-action footage still requires plenty of textures and atmospheres, and also because to blend with digital animation added later practical effects are essential).

The *Chinese Ghost Story* script was reworked, but retained most of

---
[2] Many of the same gags of the original film were included, but in slightly different places.
[3] Superstar DP Arthur Wong lit the film.

the original elements, like the hapless scholar, the beautiful ghost, the wily swordsman, and of course a clutch of monsters. The 2011 version kept the same mix of romance, humour, horror and drama (tho' the humour was much less effective, and Yu Shaoqun was not as classy a comedian as Leslie Cheung).

Inevitably, when contemplating a remake of a much-adored movie, you can't help comparing the two, and realizing that Yu Shaoqun is no Leslie Cheung, and Liu Yifei is no Joey Wong (Liu seems too contemporary a face and too insipid to inspire much heat). There was genuine romantic warmth between Cheung and Wong, which's lacking in the Yu-Liu relationship.

Truth is, if the 1987 movie (and its sequels) didn't exist, we'd be celebrating the 2011 *A Chinese Ghost Story* as a marvellous re-invention of classical, Chinese mythology and folklore. If Tsui Hark hadn't got there first (as he so often does), the 2011 movie could be seen as an innovative take on traditional, Chinese storytelling.

Among Charcoal Tan' Cheungs additions to the 1987 script written by Yuen Kai-Chi were a troubled back-story for the Taoist swordsman (plus a voiceover); adding some other monster hunters (including rivalry between them); adding Swordsman Yin having a relationship with the ghost (seen in flashbacks); multiplying the spectral creatures (so there's a whole brothel-full of ghostly monsters lurking around the temple, and the Tree Demon has two snake daughters); giving scholar Ning Choi-san a buck-toothed sidekick, called Tooth (*à la* the Wong Fei-hung films); adding a water shortage to the mountain village; and numerous computer-aided animated elements to enhance the monsters. The 2011 version also incorporates elements from the sequels to the 1987 *A Chinese Ghost Story*.

Some of the action was impressively staged in the finale of the 2011 remake, with some unusual shifts into metaphysical territory (which ghost stories are perfect for). In one gag, Swordsman Yin is swallowed by the Tree Demon, but fights for supremacy inside the monster: the struggle was visualized with very effective cuts and superimpositions from the Tree Demon to Yin in monsterish make-up. Here Yin plays the true hero by performing the ultimate sacrifice – killing himself within the Tree Demon which also means killing the monster.

Enchanting Shadow (1960).

A Chinese Ghost Story (2011).

Portrait of a Nymph (1988).

FILMOGRAPHY
TONY CHING SIU-TUNG

MOVIES AS DIRECTOR

Duel To the Death (1983)
The Witch From Nepal (1986)
A Chinese Ghost Story (1987)
The Terracotta Warrior (1989)
The Swordsman (1990 – co-directed)
A Chinese Ghost Story 2 (1990)
The Raid (1991 – co-directed)
A Chinese Ghost Story 3 (1991)
Swordsman 2 (1992)
Swordsman 3 (1993 – co-directed)
The Heroic Trio (1993, co-directed)
The Executioners (1993, co-directed)
Wonder Seven (1994)
Dr. Wai In "The Scripture With No Words" (1996)
The Longest Day (1997)
Conman In Tokyo (2000)
Naked Weapon (2002)
Belly of the Beast (2003)
An Empress and the Warriors (2008)
The Sorcerer and the White Snake (2011)
Jade Dynasty (2019)

MOVIES AS ACTION DIRECTOR

The Fourteen Amazons (1972)
The Rats (1972)
Love and Vengeance (1973)
Shaolin Boxer (1974)
The Tea House (1974)
Kidnap (1974)
Lady of the Law (1975)
Negotiation (1977)
He Who Never Dies (1979)
Monkey Kung Fu (1979)
The Bastard Swordsman (1979)
The Sentimental Swordsman (1979)
Dangerous Encounter - 1st Kind (1980)
The Spooky Bunch (1980)
The Sword (1980)
The Master Strikes (1980)
Gambler's Delight (1981)
Return of the Deadly Blade (1981)
Sword of Justice (1981)
The Story of Woo Viet (1981)
Rolls, Rolls, I Love You (1982)
Once Upon a Rainbow (1982)
Swordsman Adventure (1983)
Twinkle Twinkle Little Star (1983)
Cherie (1984)
Happy Ghost 3 (1986)
Peking Opera Blues (1986)
A Better Tomorrow 2 (1987)
The Eighth Happiness (1988)
I Love Maria (1988)
The Killer (1989)
All About Ah-Long (1989)
The Fun, the Luck and the Tycoon (1990)
Casino Raiders 2 (1991)
Son On the Run (1991)
New Dragon Gate Inn (1992 – co-directed)
Moon Warriors (1992)
Twin Dragons (1992)
Royal Tramp (1992)
Royal Tramp 2 (1992)
Gambling Soul (1992)
Justice, My Foot! (1992)
Lucky Encounter (1992)
Flying Dagger (1993)
Future Cops (1993)

Holy Weapon (1993)
The Mad Monk (1993)
Butterfly and Sword (1993)
City Hunter (1993)
Love On Delivery (1994)
A Chinese Odyssey I: Pandora's Box (1995)
A Chinese Odyssey 2: Cinderella (1995)
The Stuntwoman (1996)
Warriors of Virtue (1997)
Hong Niang (1998)
The Blacksheep Affair (1998)
The Assassin Swordsman (2000)
The Duel (2000)
My School Mate, the Barbarian (2001)
Invincible (2001)
Shaolin Soccer (2001)
Hero (2002)
Spider-Man (2002 – uncredited)
House of Flying Daggers (2004)
The Curse of the Golden Flower (2006)
Krrish (2006)
In the Name of the King: A Dungeon Siege Tale (2007)
The Warlords (2007)
Dororo (2007)
Legend of Shaolin Kungfu I: Heroes in Troubled Times (2007)
Butterfly Lovers (2008)
Kung Fu Dunk (2008)
The Treasure Hunter (2009)
Future X-Cops (2010)
Just Call Me Nobody (2010)
Legend of Shaolin Kungfu 3: Heroes of the Great Desert (2011)
Krrish 3 (2013)

TV SERIES

The Spirit of the Sword (1978)
It Takes a Thief (1979)
The Roving Swordsman (1979)
Reincarnated (1979)
Reincarnated 2 (1979)
Dynasty (1980)
Dynasty 2 (1980)
Legend of the Condor Heroes (1983)
The Return of the Condor Heroes (1983)
The New Adventures of Chor Lau Heung (1984)
The Duke of Mount Deer (1984)
The Return of Luk Siu Fung (1986)
The New Heaven Sword and Dragon Sabre (1986)
The Storm Riders (a.k.a. *Wind and Cloud*, 2002)
The Storm Riders 2 (a.k.a. *Wind and Cloud 2*, 2004)
The Royal Swordsmen (2005)

FILMOGRAPHY
TONY CHING SIU-TUNG
FILMS AS DIRECTOR

DUEL TO THE DEATH, 1983

(A.k.a. *Sang Sei Kyu/ Sheng Si Jue*). Production: Paragon Films. Distributor: Golden Harvest. Producers: Raymond Chow Man-Wai and Catherine Chang Si-kan. Script: David Lai, Manfred Wong and Ching Siu-tung. Released: Jan 13, 1983. 86 mins.

THE WITCH FROM NEPAL, 1986

(*Qi Yuan* in Mandarin, a.k.a. *The Nepal Affair/ Affair From Nepal/ A Touch of Love*). Production: Golden Harvest/ Paragon Films. Producer: Anthony Chow. Script: Chui Jing-Hong. Released: Feb 27, 1986. 89 mins.

A CHINESE GHOST STORY, 1987

(Mandarin: *Qiannu Youhun = Sien: Female Ghost*, a.k.a. *Fair Maiden, Tender Spirit*). Production: Film Workshop/ Cinema City. Producers: Tsui Hark, Claudie Chung Jan and Qianqing Liu. Exec. producer: Zhong Zheng. Script: Yuen Kai-Chi. Released: July 18, 1987. 98 mins.

THE TERRACOTTA WARRIOR, 1989

(*Chin Yung/ Gu Gam Daai Zin/ Yon Qing* in Cantonese, a.k.a. *Fight and Love With a Terracotta Warrior*). Production: Art & Talent Group Inc. Exec. producer: Kam Kwok-Leung. Producers: Tsui Hark, Zhu Mu and Hon Pau-chu. Script: Pik Wah Lee. Released: Apl 12, 1990. 106 mins. (145 mins).

THE SWORDSMAN, 1990

(Cantonese = *Siu Ngo Gong Woo*, Mandarin = *Xiao Aoi Jianzhu* = *Laughing and Proud Warrior*). Production: Film Workshop/ Golden Harvest. Producers: Tsui Hark, Tommy Law Wai-Tak and Chu Feng Kang. Script: Kwan Man-Leung, Daai Foo Ho, Huang Ying, Tai-Mok Lau, Yiu-ming Leung, and Jason Lam Kee To. Co-directed with Raymond Lee, King Hu, Tsui Hark, Andrew Kam Yeung-Wa and Ann Hui. Released: Apl 5, 1990. 115 mins.

A CHINESE GHOST STORY 2, 1990

(Mandarin: *Qiannü Youhun Zhi Renjian Dao = Sien Female Ghost II: Human Realm Tao*). Production: Film Workshop/ Golden Princess. Producer: Tsui Hark. Script: Lau Tai-mok, Lam Kei-to and Leung Yiu-ming. Story: Tsui Hark and Yuen Kai-Chi. Released: July 13, 1990. 98/ 104 mins.

THE RAID, 1991

(*Choi Suk Ji Wang Siu Chin Gwan*). Production: Film Workshop and Cinema City. Producer: Tsui Hark. Script: Tsui Hark and Yuen Kai-chi. Story: Michael Hui Koon-Man. Co-directed with Tsui Hark. Released: Mch 28, 1991. 100 mins.

A CHINESE GHOST STORY 3, 1991

(*Qiannü Youhun III Dao Dao Dao*). Production: Golden Princess/ Film Workshop. Exec. producers: Chui Bo-Chu and Roger Lee Yan-Lam. Producer: Tsui Hark. Co-producer: Cho King-Man. Script: Roy Szeto Cheuk-hon and Tsui Hark. Released: July 18, 1991. 99 mins.

THE SWORDSMAN 2, 1992

(Cantonese: *Siu Ngo Kong Woo II Dong Fong Bat Baai;* Mandarin: *Xiao-ao Jianghu II Dongfang Bubai = Laughing and Proud Warrior: Invincible Asia*). Production: Film Workshop/ Long Shong Pictures/ Golden Princess. Producer: Tsui Hark. Assoc. producers: Chi-Wai Cheung and Wai Sum Shia. Script: Hanson Chan Tin-suen, Elsa Tang Pik-yin and Tsui Hark. Released: June 26, 1992. 108 mins.

THE SWORDSMAN 3, 1993

(A.k.a. *The East Is Red.* Mandarin: *Dongfang Bùbài – Fengyún Zàiqi = Invisible Asia 3: Turbulence Again Rises*). Production: Film Workshop/ Long Shong Pictures/ Golden Princess. Producers: Tsui Hark and Lau Jou. Script: Tsui Hark, Charcoal Tan Cheung and Roy Szeto Chak-Hon. Co-directed with Raymond Lee Wai-man. Released: Jan 21, 1993. 93 minutes.

THE HEROIC TRIO, 1993

(*Dung Fong Saam Hap*). Production: China Entertainment Films and Paka Hill Productions. Producer: Tony Ching. Script: Sandy Shaw Lai-King. Co-directed with Johnny To Ke-fung. Released: Feb 12, 1993. 83 mins.

THE EXECUTIONERS, 1993

(*Xian Dai Hao Xia Zhuan*, a.k.a. *The Heroic Trio 2*). Production: China Entertainment Films and Paka Hill Film. Producers: Johnnie To Ke-fung, Tony Ching and Yeung Kwok-fai. Script: Susanne Chan and Sandy Shaw Lai-King. Co-directed with Johnnie To Ke-fung. Released: Sept 30, 1993. 97 mins.

WONDER SEVEN, 1994

(*7 Jin Gong*). Production: China Entertainment Films. Producer: Catherine Hun. Script: Charcoal Tan Cheung, Elsa Tang Bikyin and Tony Ching. Story: Manfred Wong Man-Chun. Released: Apl 1, 1994. 88 mins.

DR WAI IN "THE SCRIPTURE WITH NO WORDS", 1996

(*Yale: Mo Him Wong,* a.k.a. *Mao Xian Wang*). Production: Win's Entertainment and Eastern Production. Producers: Tsai Mu-ho, Wong Sing-ping, Charles Heung Wah-keung and Tiffany Chen Ming-Ying. Script: Lam Wai-Lun, Roy Szeto Cheuk-hon and Sandy Shaw Lai-King. Released: Mch 14, 1996. 87/ 91 mins.

CONMAN IN TOKYO, 2000

(*Zung Waa Dou Hap*). Production: Star East and Best of the Best and Partners. Producer: Wong Jing. Script: Law Yiu-fai. Released: Aug 31, 2000. 103 mins.

NAKED WEAPON, 2002

(*Chek Law Dak Gung*). Production: Media Asia/ Jing Productions. Producers: Wong Jing and John Chong. Script: Wong Jing. Released: Nov 15, 2002. 92 mins.

BELLY OF THE BEAST, 2003

Production: G.F.T. Entertainment/ Salon Films/ Studio Eight Productions/ Emmett/ Furla Films. Producers: George Furla, Gary Howsam, Jamie Brown, Randall Emmett, Steven Seagal and Charles Wang. Script: Thomas Fenton and James Townsend. Released: Dec 30,

2003. 91 mins.

AN EMPRESS AND THE WARRIORS, 2008

(*Jiang Shan Mei Ren* = *The Kingdom and a Beauty*). Production: Beijing Polyabana Publishing Co./ United Filmmakers Organization/ China Film Co-Production Corp./ Big Pictures, Ltd. Execuive producers: Eric Tsang and Kuo Hsing Li. Producers: Claudie Chung Jan, Gin Lau Sin-hing, Peter Chan and Dong Yu. Script: James Yuen, Charcoal Tan Cheung and Tin Nam Chun. Released: Mch 19, 2008. 99 mins.

THE SORCERER AND THE WHITE SNAKE, 2011

(*Baak Se Cyun Syut Zi Faat Hoi*, a.k.a. *The Emperor and the White Snake*, a.k.a. *Madame White Snake*, a.k.a. *It's Love*). Production: China Juli Entertainment Media/ Distribution Workshop/ Different Digital Design Ltd. Exec. producer: Pang Yau-Fong. Producers: Chui Po Chu, Chi Wan Tse and Yang Zi. Script: Charcoal Tan Cheung, Tsang Kan Cheung and Roy Szeto Cheuk-hon. Released: Sept 28, 2011. 100 mins.

JADE DYNASTY, 2019

(*Zhu Xian*). Production: Huxia Film Distribution/ New Classics Pictures/ Shanghai Taopiaopiao Film Culture/ Youku Pictures/ I.Q.I.Y.I. Pictures. Producer: Ning Li. Line producers: Huang Qunfei, Jia Xu and Tony Ching. Script: Shen Jie and Song Chaoyun. Released: Sept 13, 2019. 101 mins.

TONY CHING SIU-TUNG

FILMS AS ACTION DIRECTOR

THE SWORD, 1980

(*Jian* a.k.a. *Ming Jian*). Production: Golden Harvest. Producer: Raymond Chow Man-Wai. Script: Lau Shing-Hon, Clifford Choi Gai-Gwong, Wong Ying, Patrick Tam Kar-Ming, Lo Chi-Keung and Lau Tin-Chi. Direction: Patrick Tam Kar-ming. Released: Aug 14, 1980. 84 mins.

DANGEROUS ENCOUNTER – 1ST KIND, 1980

(*Diyi Leixing Weixian = First Kind of Danger*, a.k.a. *Dangerous Encounter of the First Kind*, *Don't Play With Fire* and *Playing With Fire*). Production: Fotocine Film Production Ltd. Producer: Thomas Wing-Fat Fung. Script: Tsui Hark and Roy Szeto Cheuk-hon. Direction: Tsui Hark. Released: Dec 4, 1980. 92 mins.

TWINKLE TWINKLE LITTLE STAR, 1983

(*Xing Ji Dun Tai*). Production: Shaw Brothers. Producer: by Mona Fong Yat-wah. Script: Alex Cheung Kwok-ming, Manfred Wong Man-jun, John Au Wa-hon, Sandy Shaw Lai-king, Lawrence Cheng Tan-shui and Yuen Gai-chi. Direction: Alex Cheung Kwok-ming. Released: Feb 12, 1983. 93 mins.

PEKING OPERA BLUES, 1986

(*Dao Ma Dan = Knife Horse Actresses*). Production: Cinema City/ Film Workshop. Producers: Claudie Chung-jan and Tsui Hark. Script: Raymond To Kwok-wai. Direction: Tsui Hark. Released: Sept 6, 1986. 104 mins.

A BETTER TOMORROW 2, 1987

(*Jing Hung Bun Sik II* in Cantonese, *Ying Xiong Ben Se II* in Mandarin = *Heroic Character II*). Production: Cinema City. Producer: Tsui Hark. Script: Tsui Hark and John Woo. Direction: John Woo (Ng Yu-sam). Released: Dec 17, 1987. 104 mins.

I LOVE MARIA, 1988

(*Roboforce*). Producers: Tsui Hark and John Sham. Script: Yuen Kai-chi. Direction: David Chung Chi-man. Released: Mch 10, 1988. 96 mins.

THE KILLER, 1989

(*Dip Huet Seung Hung* in Cantonese, *Die Xue Shuang Xiong* in Mandarin = *Bloodshed Brothers*, 1989). Production: Film Workshop/ Golden Princess/ Magnum. Script: John Woo. Producer: Tsui Hark. Direction: John Woo. Released: July 6, 1989. 105 mins.

JUST HEROES, 1989

(A.k.a. *Tragic Heroes*, *Yi Dan Qun Ying* in Cantonese). Production by Magnum Films. Producers: Alan Ng, David Chiang, Danny Lee, and Tsui Hark. Exec. prod. by Chang Cheh. Script: Ni Kuang, Tommy Hau and Yiu Yau Hung. Direction: John Woo and Wu Ma. Released: Sept 14, 1989. 97 mins.

THE BANQUET, 1991

(*Hao Men Ye Yan*). Producers: Ng See-yuen and John Sham. Script: Choi Ting-ting. Direction: Clifton Ko-chi, Alfred Sum, Joe Tin, Kin Cheung and Tung Cheung Cho. Released: Nov 30, 1991. 97 mins.

NEW DRAGON GATE INN, 1992

(*Xin Long Menm Ke Zhan* in Mandarin). Production: Film Workshop and Seasonal Films. Producers: Tsui Hark and Ng See-yuen. Script: Tsui Hark, Charcoal Tan Cheung and Hiu Wing. Direction: Raymond Lee Wai-man and Tsui Hark. Released: by Aug 27, 1992. 103 mins.

CITY HUNTER, 1993

(*Sing Si Lip Ya*). Production: Golden Harvest/ Golden Way Films/ Paragon Films. Producer: Chua Lam. Script and direction: Wong Jing. Released: Jan 14, 1993. 105 mins.

THE MAD MONK, 1993

(*Ji Gong*). Production: Cosmopolitan Film Productions. Producer: Mona Fong Yat-wah. Script: Sandy Shaw Lai-king. Direction: Johnnie To Ke-fung. Released: July 29, 1993. 85 mins.

FUTURE COPS, 1993

(*Chiu Kap Hok Hau Ba Wong*). Production: Wong Jing's Workshop and Fantasy Productions Inc.. Producers: John Higgins and Sherman Wong Shui-Hin. Script and direction: Wong Jing. Released: July 15, 1993. 95 mins.

LOVE ON DELIVERY, 1994

(*Po Huai Zhi Wang*, a.k.a. *King Of Destruction*). Production: Cosmopolitan Films. Script: Vincent Kok Tak-chiu. Direction: Stephen Chow Sing-chi and Lee Lik-Chi. Some credits have Tony Ching as co-director with Lee. Released: Feb 3, 1994. 100 mins.

A CHINESE ODYSSEY, 1995

(*Daiwah Saiyau* and *Sai Yau Gei: Daai Git Guk Ji-Sin Leui Kei Yun*). Production: Xi'an Film Studio and Choi Sing Film Company. Producer: Yeung Kwok-fai. Script: Wu Cheng-en. Direction: Jeffrey Lau. Released: Jan 21, 1995 and Feb 4, 1995. 87 and 95 mins.

WARRIOR OF VIRTUE, 1997

(*Wu Xing Zhan Shi*). Production: Joseph, Ronald, Dennis K., Jeremy and Christopher Law, Yoram Barzilai, Lyle Howry and Patricia Ruben. Distribution: Metro Goldwyn Mayer. Script: Michael Vickerman and Hugh Kelley. Direction: Ronny Yu. Released: May 2, 1997. 101 mins.

BLACKSHEEP AFFAIR, 1998

(*Meltdown 2, Another Meltdown* and *Bi Xie Lan Tian*). Production: Win's Entertainment/ Eastern Film Production. Producer: Alex Law Kai-yui. Presenters: Charles Heung Wah-keung and Chui Po-chu. Script: Roy Szeto Cheuk-hon and Alex Law. Direction: Lam Wai-lun. Released: Feb 14, 1998. 90 mins.

THE DUEL, 2000

(*Jue Zhan Zi Jin Zhi Dian*). Production: Win's Entertainment. Producers: Wong Jing and Manfred Wong. Script: Manfred Wong. Direction: Andy Lau Wai-keung. Released: Feb 3, 2000. 106 mins.

SHAOLIN SOCCER, 2001

(*Siu Lam* in Cantonese, *Shàolín Zúqiú* in Mandarin). Production: Universe Entertainment and Star Overseas. Producer: Yeung Kwok-Fai. Script: Tsang Kan-cheung and Stephen Chow Sing-chi. Direction: Lee Lik-chi and Stephen Chow. Released: July 12, 2001. 112 mins.

INVINCIBLE, 2001

Production: T.B.S. Producers: Steven Chasman, Janine Coughlin and Jim Lemley. Executive producers: Bruce Davey, Mel Gibson, Jet Li, and John Morayniss. Script: Carey Hayes, Chad Hayes, Michael Brandt, Derek Haas, and Jefrey Levy. Direction: Jefrey Levy. Released: Nov 18, 2001. 87 mins.

SPIDER-MAN, 2002

Production: Marvel/ Columbia/ Laura Ziskin Prods. Producers: Laura Ziskin and Ian Bryce. Script: David Koepp. Direction: Sam Raimi. Released: May 3, 2002. 121 mins.

HERO, 2002

(Mandarin: *Yingxiong;* Cantonese: *Jing Hung*). Production: China Film Co-Production Corporation/ Elite Group Enterprises/ Zhang Yimou Studio/ Metropole Organisation/ Miramax Films/ Beijing New Picture Film. Executive producers: Shoufang Dou and Weiping Zhang. Producers: Bill Kong, Sook Yhun and Zhang Yimou. Script: Feng Li, Zhang Yimou and Bin Wang. Direction: Zhang Yimou. Released: Oct 24, 2002. 99 mins.

HOUSE OF FLYING DAGGERS, 2004

(*Shí Miàn Mái Fú*). Production: China Film Co-Production Corporation/ E.D.K.O. Films/ Elite Group/ Zhang Yimou Studio/ Beijing New Pictures. Executive producer: Weiping Zhang. Producers: Bill Kong, Zhenyan Zhang and Zhang Yimou. Script: Bin Wang, Li Feng, Peter Wu and Zhang Yimou. Direction: Zhang Yimou. Released: July 15, 2004. 119 mins.

KRRISH, 2006

Production: Filmkraft Productions. Producer: Rakesh Roshan. Script: Sanjay Masoomi, Sachin Bhowmick, Rakesh Roshan, Akash Khurana, Honey Irani and Robin Bhatt. Direction: Rakesh Roshan. Released: June 23, 2006. 175 mins.

CURSE OF THE GOLDEN FLOWER, 2006

(*Manchéng Jìndài Huángjinjia*, a.k.a. *The City of Golden Armor,* a.k.a. *Autumn Remembrance*). Production: E.D.K.O. Film/ Bejing New Pictures Film/ Elite Group Enterprises. Producers: Zhang Weiping, Bill Kong and Zhang Yimou. Script: Zhihong Bian, Nan Wu, and Zhang Yimou. Direction: Zhang Yimou. Released: Dec 21, 2006. 114 mins.

THE WARLORDS, 2007

(*Tau Ming Song* a.k.a. *The Blood Brothers*). Production: Media Asia/ China Film Group/ Morgan & Chan. Producers: Andre Morgan and Peter Chan. Script: Xu Lan, Chun Tin-nam, Aubery Lam, Huang Jianxin, Jojo Hui, He Jiping, Guo Junli and James Yuen. Direction: Peter Chan. Released: Dec 12, 2007. 127 mins.

IN THE NAME OF THE KING, 2007

Production: Brightlight Pictures/ Boll K.G. Productions/ Herold Productions. Producers: Dan Clarke, Shawn Williamson, Uwe Boll and Wolfgang Herold. Script: Doug Taylor. Direction: Uwe Boll. Released: April 11, 2007. 127 mins.

DORORO, 2007

Production: Toho/ Tokyo Broadcasting System/ Twins Japan/ Yahoo Japan/ W.O.W.O.W./ Universal/ Dentsu/ Mainichi Broadcasting System/ Hokkaido Broadcasting Company/ Asahi Shimbun/ Stardust Pictures. Producers: Takashi Hirano and Atsuyuki Shimoda. Script: Osamu Tezuka, Masa Nakamura and Akihiko Shiota. Direction: Akihiko Shiota. Released: Mch 15, 2007. 139 mins.

THE BUTTERFLY LOVERS, 2008

(*Jian Die*). Production: Brilliant Idea Group/ China Film Co-Production Corp./ Xian Mei Ah Culture Communciation Ltd. Producer: Catherine Hun. Script: Chris Ng Ka-keung, Yeung Sin-ling, Wong Nga-man, Jingle Ma Choh-shing and Chan Po-chun. Direction: Jingle Ma Choh-shing. Released: Oct 9, 2008. 102 mins.

KUNG FU DUNK, 2008

(*Gonfu* or *Guanlan* in Cantonese). Production: Shanghai Film Group/ Emperor Motion Pictures/ MediaCorp Raintree. Executive producers: Albert Yeung, Zhonglun Ren and Wu Tun. Producers: Zhao Xiaoding, Pengle Xu, Albert Lee and Yiu Kay Wah. Script: Kevin Chu Yen Ping, You-Chen Wang and Lam Chiu Wing. Direction: Kevin Chu Yen-ping. Released:

Feb 7, 2008. 98 mins.

THE TREASURE HUNTER, 2009

(*Ci Lung*). Production: Chang Hong Channel Film & Video. Producers: Han Sanping, Han Xiaoli, Jiang Tai, Raymond Lee, Pei Gin-yam, Du Yang, Ding Li, Dong Zhengrong and Han Xiao. Script: Charcoal Cheung Tan, Yip Wan-chiu, Lam Chiu-wing, Lam Ching-yan and Shao Huiting. Direction: Kevin Chu Yen-ping. Released: Dec 9, 2009. 105 mins.

FUTURE X-COPS, 2010

(*Wei Lai Jing Cha*). Production: China Film Group Corp. Producers: Ken Nickel, Haicheng Zhao, Ming Li, Sanping Han, Jason Han and Venus Keung. Direction and script: Wong Jing. Released: Apl 15, 2010. 101 mins.

THE IRON FORT'S FURIOUS LION, 2010

(*Irumbukkottai Murattu Singam*). Production: A.G.S. Entertainment. Producers: Kalpathi S. Aghoram, Kalpathi S. Ganesh and Kalpathi S. Suresh. Script and direction: Chimbu Deven. Released: May 7, 2010. 140 mins.

JUST CALL ME NOBODY, 2010

(*Da Xiao Jiang Hu*). Production: Polybona Film Distribution Co.,Ltd. Producers: Kevin Chu Yen-ping, Don Yu-dong, Maxx Tsai, Jeffrey Chan and Zhao Benshan. Script: Ning Cai Shen. Direction Kevin Chu Yen-ping. Released: Dec 3, 2010. 94 mins.

KRRISH 3, 2013

Production: Filmkraft Productions. Executive producer: Shammi Saini. Producers: Sunaina Roshan and Rakesh Roshan. Script: Rakesh Roshan, Akash Khurana, Honey Irani, Sanjay Masoomi, Irfan Kamal, David Benullo, Rajshri Sudhakar and Robin Bhatt. Direction: Rakesh Roshan. Released: Nov 1, 2013. 152 mins.

RECOMMENDED BOOKS AND WEBSITES

One of the finest general introductions to the history of Hong Kong cinema, and a great place to start, is *Hong Kong Cinema* (1997) by Stephen Teo. David Bordwell and Kristin Thompson are consistently excellent commentators on film, in books such as *Film History: An Introduction* (2010) and Bordwell's account of Hong Kong cinema, *Planet Hong Kong: Popular Cinema and the Art of Entertainment* (2000).

Bey Logan's *Hong Kong Action Cinema* (1995) is an entertaining introduction to the action side of Hong Kong cinema (with many valuable illustrations). *Kung-fu Cult Masters: From Bruce Lee To 'Crouching Tiger'* (2003) takes a more theoretical approach to the same subject.

For surveys of films, Jeff Yang's *Once Upon a Time In China* (2003) is superb, as is *Hong Kong Babylon* (1997) by F. Dannen & B. Long (this book also features many interviews with the key players in the Hong Kong industry). Lisa Morton's *The Cinema of Tsui Hark* (2001) is an important early study.

Jackie Chan has attracted many studies and biographies, including *Jackie Chan* by C. Gentry (1997), *The Essential Jackie Chan Sourcebook* by J. Rovin & K. Tracy (1997), and *Dying For Action: The Life and Times of Jackie Chan* by R. Witterstaetter (1997). And Chan's own memoirs: *I Am Jackie Chan* (1998) and *Never Grow Up* (2018).

Among critical essays, I would recommend *At Full Speed: Hong Kong Cinema In a Borderless World* (1998, edited by E.C.M. Yau) and *The Cinema of Hong Kong* (2002), edited by P. Fu & D. Desser.

WEBSITES

Hong Kong Movie Database
Love Hong Kong Film
Hong Kong Cinemagic
Film Workshop
Jet Li   jetli.com

BIBLIOGRAPHY

ON TSUI HARK

B. Accomando. "Army of Darkness: Hong Kong Director Tsui Hark Takes On the West", *Giant Robot*, 8, 1997
G. Hendrix. "Tsui Hark: Great Directors", *Senses of Cinema*, July, 2013
Howard Hampton. "Once Upon a Time In Hong Kong", *Film Comment*, 33, 1997
Hal Hinson. "*Peking Opera Blues*," *Washington Post*, Oct 14, 1988
D. Houx. "The Underrated Insanity of Tsui Hark and Jean-Claude van Damme's *Knock Off*', *Badass Digest,* 2014
A. Hwang. "The Irresistible: Hong Kong Movie *Once Upon a Time In China* Series", *Asian Cinema*, 10, 1, 1998
Y. Lee. "Artist Provocateur – On Tsui Hark", Hong Kong International Film Festival, 23, 1999
P. Macias. "Animerica Interview: Tsui Hark", *Animerica*, 7, 10
The Making of A Chinese Ghost Story: The Tsui Hark Animation, Hong Kong, 1997
L. Morton. *The Cinema of Tsui Hark*, McFarland, Jefferson, North Carolina, 2001
C. Reid. "Interview With Tsui Hark", *Film Quarterly*, 48, 3, 1995
S. Short. "Tsui Hark", interview, *Time*, CNN, 2000
Chuck Stephens. "Tsui Hark's Planet Hong Kong", *Village Voice*, May 1, 2001
S. Tan. "Ban(g)! Ban(g)! *Dangerous Encounter – 1st Kind*', *Asian Cinema*, 8, 1, 1996
Stephen Teo. "Tsui Hark: Filmography", *Senses of Cinema* 17, Nov, 2001
Tsui Hark. Interview, in F. Dannen, 1997
Ben Umstead. "An Interview With Tsui Hark", *Twitch*/ N.Y.A.F.F., 2011, July 11, 2011

OTHERS

A. Abbas. *Hong Kong*, University of Minnoestoa Press, Minneapolis, 1997
J. Abert. *A Knight At the Movies: Medieval History On Film*, Routledge, London, 2003
G. Adair. *Vietnam on Film*, Proteus, New York, NY, 1981
—. *Hollywood's Vietnam*, Heinemann, London, 1989
R.C. Allen, ed. *Channels of Discourse: Television and Contemporary Criticism*, Methuen, London, 1987
R. Altman, ed. *Sound Theory, Sound Practice*, Routledge, London, 1992
—. *Film/ Genre*, British Film Institute, London, 1999
M. Anderegg, ed. *Inventing Vietnam*, Temple University Press, Philadelphia, PA, 1991
G. Andrew. *The Film Handbook*, Longman, London, 1989
—. *Stranger Than Paradise: Maverick Filmmakers In Recent American Cinema*, Prion, 1998
A. Assister & A. Carol, eds. *Bad Girls and Dirty Pictures: The Challenge To Reclaim Feminism*, Pluto Press, London, 1993
A. Auster. *How the War Was Remembered: Hollywood and Vietnam*, Praeger, New York, NY, 1988
R. Baker & T. Russell. *The Essential Guide To Hong Kong Movies*, Eastern Heroes, London, 1994
—. *The Essential Guide To the Best of Eastern Heroes*, Eastern Heroes, London, 1995
—. *The Essential Guide To Deadly China Dolls*, Eastern Heroes, London, 1996
M. Barker, ed. *The Video Nasties: Freedom and Censorship In the Media*, Pluto Press, London, 1984
—. & J. Petley, eds. *Ill Effects: The Media/ Violence Debate*, Routledge, London, 1997
L. Bawden, ed. *The Oxford Companion To Film*, Oxford University Press, Oxford, 1976
J. Baxter. *George Lucas*, HarperCollins, London, 1999
J. Beck, ed. *Animation Art*, Flame Tree Publishing, London, 2004

M. Beja. *Film and Literature: An Introduction*, Longman, London, 1979
R. Bergan & R. Karney. *Bloomsbury Foreign Film Guide*, Bloomsbury, London, 1988
I. Bergman. *Talking With Ingmar Bergman*, Dallas, TX, 1983
—. *Bergman on Bergman, Interviews with Ingmar Bergman*, eds. S. Björkman, *et al*, tr. P. B. Austin, Touchstone, New York, NY, 1986
—. *The Magic Lantern: An Autobiography*, London, 1988
C. Berry. *Perspectives On Chinese Cinema*, B.F.I., London, 1991
P. Biskind. *Easy Riders, Raging Bulls: How the Sex 'n' Drugs 'n' Rock 'n' Roll Generation Saved Hollywood*, Bloomsbury, London, 1998
—. *Down and Dirty Pictures: Miramax, Sundance and the Rise of Independent Film*, Bloomsbury, London, 2004
M. Bliss. *Between the Bullets: The Spiritual Cinema of John Woo*, Scarecrow Press, Lanham, MD, 2002
A. Block & L. Wilson, eds. *George Lucas's Blockbusting*, HarperCollins, New York, 2010
D. Bordwell & K. Thompson. *Film Art: An Introduction*, McGraw-Hill Publishing Company, New York, NY, 1979
—. *et al. The Classical Hollywood Cinema: Film Style and Mode of Production To 1960*, Routledge, London, 1985
—. *Narration In the Fiction Film*, Routledge, London, 1988
—. *Making Meaning*, Harvard University Press, Cambridge, MA, 1989
—. & N. Caroll, eds. *Post-Theory: Reconstructing Film Studies*, University of Wisconsin Press, Madison, WI, 1996
—. *Planet Hong Kong: Popular Cinema and the Art of Entertainment*, Harvard University Press, 2000
—. "Aesthetics in Action: *Kungfu*, Gunplay and Cinematic Expressivity", in E. Yau, 2001
—. *The Way Hollywood Tells It*, University of California Press, Berkeley, CA, 2006
J. Bower, ed. *The Cinema of Japan and Korea*, Wallflower Press, London, 2004
D. Breskin. *Inner Voices: Filmmakers In Conversation*, Da Capo, New York, 1997
A. Britton *et al*. *American Nightmare: Essays On the Horror Film*, Toronto, 1979
A. Brown. *Directing Hong Kong: The Political Cinema of John Woo and Wong Kar-Wai*, Routledge/ Curzon, 2001
R. Brown. *Overtones and Undertones: Reading Film Music*, University of California Press, Berkeley, CA, 1994
N. Browne *et al*, eds. *New Chinese Cinema*, Cambridge University Press, 1994
S. Bukatman. *Terminal Identity: The Virtual Subject In Postmodern Science Fiction*, Duke University Press, Durham, NC, 1993
G. Burt. *The Art of Film Music*, Northeastern University Press, 1994
B. Camp & J. Davis. *Anime Classics*, Stone Bridge Press, CA, 2007
J. Campbell. *The Power of Myth*, with B. Moyers, ed. B.S. Flowers, Doubleday, New York, NY, 1988
J. Chan. *I Am Jackie Chan*, with Jeff Yang, Pan Books, 1998
—. *Never Grow Up*, Simon & Schuster, London, 2018
J. Charles. *The Hong Kong Filmography: 1977-1997*, McFarland, 2000
R. Chu. "*Swordman II* and *The East Is Red*", *Bright Lights*, 13, 1994
C. Chun-shu & Shelley Hsueh-lun Chang. *Redefining History: Ghosts, Spirits, and Human Society in Pu Sung-ling's World, 1640–1715*, University of Michigan Press, Ann Arbor, 1998
D. Chute & Cheng-Sim Lim, eds. *Heroic Grace: The Chinese Martial Arts Film*, University of California, Los Angeles, Film and Television Archive, 2003
P. Clark. *Chinese Cinema: Culture and Politics Since 1949*, Cambridge University Press, 1987
J. Clements & H. McCarthy, eds. *The Anime Encyclopedia*, Stone Bridge Press, Berkeley, CA, 2001/ 2007/ 2015
S. Cohan & I.R. Hark, eds. *Screening the Male: Exploring Masculinities In Hollywood Cinema*, Routledge, London, 1993
J. Collins *et al*, eds. *Film Theory Goes To the Movies*, Routledge, New York, NY, 1993
D.A. Cook. *A History of Narrative Film*, W.W. Norton, New York, NY, 1981, 1990, 1996
P. Cook, ed. *The Cinema Book*, British Film Institute, London, 1985/ 1999
S. Cornelius & I. Smith. *New Chinese Cinema*, Wallflower Press, London, 2002
J. Crist, ed. *Take 22: Moviemakers On Moviemaking*, Continuum, New York, NY, 1991
F. Dannen & B. Long. *Hong Kong Babylon*, Faber, London, 1997
G. Deleuze & F. Guattari. *Cinema 1: The Movement Image*, Athlone Press, London, 1989
—. *Cinema 2: The Time Image*, Athlone Press, London, 1989
C. Desjardins. *Outlaw Masters of Japanese Film*, I.B. Tauris, London, 2005
D. Desser. *Eros Plus Massacre: An Introduction to the Japanese New Wave Cinema*, Indiana University Press, Bloomington, IN, 1988
L. Dittmar & G. Michael. *From Hanoi To Hollywood*, Rutgers University Press, NJ, 1991
J. Donald, ed. *Fantasy and the Cinema*, British Film Institute, London, 1989
K.J. Donnelly, ed. *Film Music*, Edinburgh University Press, Edinburgh, 2001
C. Ducker & Stuart Cutler. *The H.K.S. Guide To Jet Li*, Hong Kong Superstars, London, 2000
M. Eagleton, ed. *Feminist Literary Theory: A Reader*, Blackwell, Oxford, 1986

—. ed. *Feminist Literary Criticism*, Longman, London, 1991
A. Easthope, ed. *Contemporary Film Theory*, Longman, London, 1993
P. Ettedgui. *Production Design & Art Direction*, RotoVision, 1999
D. Fairservice. *Film Editing*, Manchester University Press, Manchester, 2001
K. Fang. *John Woo's A Better Tomorrow, The New Hong Kong Cinema*, Hong Kong University Press, Hong Kong, 2004
C. Finch. *Special Effects*, Abbeville, 1984
J. Finler. *The Movie Director's Story*, Octopus Books, London, 1985
—. *The Hollywood Story*, Wallflower Press, London, 2003
C. Fleming. *High Concept: Don Simpson and the Hollywood Culture of Excess*, Bloomsbury, London, 1998
J. Fletcher & A. Benjamin, eds. *Abjection, Melancholia and Love: The Work of Julia Kristeva*, Routledge, London, 1990
K. Fowkes. *Giving Up the Ghost: Spirits, Ghosts and Angels In Mainstream Comedy Films*, Wayne State University Press, Detroit, MI, 1998
A. Frank. *Horror Films*, Hamlyn, London, 1977
—. *The Horror Film Handbook*, Barnes & Noble, 1982
K. French, ed. *Screen Violence*, Bloomsbury, London, 1996
P. Fu & D. Desser, eds. *The Cinema of Hong Kong*, Cambridge University Press, Cambridge, 2002
Lisa Funnell. *Warrior Women: Gender, Race, and the Transnational Chinese Action Star*, State University of New York Press, 2014
M. Gallagher. "Masculinity In Translation: Jackie Chan", *Velvet Light Trap*, 39, 1997
—. *Tony Leung Chiu-wai*, British Film Instititute, 2018
L. Gamman & M. Marshment, eds. *The Female Gaze: Women as Viewers of Popular Culture*, Women's Press, London, 1988
J. Geiger & R. Rutsky, eds. *Film Analysis*, Norton & Company, New York, NY, 2005
K. Gelder & S. Thornton, eds. *The Subcultures Reader*, Routledge, London, 1997
—. ed. *The Horror Reader*, Routledge, London, 2000
J. Gelmis. *The Film Director as Superstar*, Penguin, London, 1974
C. Gentry. *Jackie Chan*, Taylor, Dallas, TX, 1997
Jean-Luc Godard. *Godard on Godard*, eds. J. Narobi & T. Milne, Da Capo, New York, NY, 1986
—. *Interviews*, ed. D. Sterritt, University of Mississippi Press, Jackson, 1998
L . Goldberg et al, eds. *Science Fiction Filmmaking In the 1980s*, McFarland, Jefferson, 1995
M. Goodwin & N. Wise. *On the Edge: The Life and Times of Francis Coppola*, William Morrow, New York, NY, 1989
B.K. Grant, ed. *Film Genre*, Scarecrow Press, Metuchen, NJ, 1977
—. ed. *Planks of Reason: Essays on the Horror Film*, Scarecrow Press, Metuchen, NJ, 1984
—. *Film Genre Reader II*, University of Texas Press, Austin, TX, 1995
—. ed. *The Dread of Difference: Gender and the Horror Film*, University of Texas Press, Austin, TX, 1996
E. Grosz. *Sexual Subversions*, Allen & Unwin, London, 1989
—. *Jacques Lacan: A Feminist Introduction*, Routledge, London, 1990
—. *Volatile Bodies*, Indiana University Press, Bloomington, IN, 1994
—. *Space, Time and Perversion*, Routledge, London, 1995
K. Hall. *John Woo: The Films*, McFarland & Co., Jefferson, N.C., 1999
L. Halliwell. *Halliwell's Filmgoer's Companion*, 7th edition, Granada, London, 1980
D. Hamamoto & S. Liu, eds. *Countervision: Asian-American Film Criticism*, Temple University Press, Philadelphia, PA, 2000
S. Hammond. *Hollywood East*, Contemporary Books, Lincoln, IL, 2000
P. Hardy, ed. *The Aurum Encyclopedia of Science Fiction*, Aurum, London, 1991
C. Heard. *Ten Thousand Bullets: The Cinematic Journey of John Woo*, Lone Eagle Publishing Co., L.A., 2000
S. & N. Hibbin. *The Official James Bond Movie Book*, Hamlyn, London, 1989
G. Hickenlooper. *Reel Conversations: Candid Interviews With Film's Foremost Directors and Critics*, Citadel, New York, NY, 1991
J. Hillier. *The New Hollywood*, Studio Vista, London, 1992
—. *American Independent Cinema: A Sight & Sound Reader*, British Film Institute, London, 2001
L.C. Hillstrom, ed. *International Dictionary of Films and Filmmakers: Directors*, St James Press, London, 1997
Sam Ho, ed. *The Swordsman and His Juang Hu: Tsui Hark and Hong Kong Film*, Hong Kong University Press, Hong Kong, 2002
Hong Kong Film Archive. *The Making of Martial Arts Films*, Hong Kong Provisional Urban Council, 1999
Hong Kong International Film Festival. *Hong Kong Panorama*, Leisure and Cultural Services Department
Hong Kong International Film Festival. *Hong Kong New Wave: Twenty Years After*, Provisional Urban Council of Hong Kong, 1999

Hong Kong International Film Festival. *Hong Kong Cinema '79-'89*, Leisure and Cultural Services Department, 2000
D. Hudson. *Draculas, Vampires, and Other Undead Forms*, Rowman & Littlefield, 2009
D. Hughes. *Comic Book Movies*, Virgin, London, 2003
L. Hughes. *The Rough Guide To Gangster Movies*, Penguin, 2005
L. Hunt. "Once Upon a Time In China: Kung Fu From Bruce Lee To Jet Li", *Framework*, 40, 1999
—. *Kung-fu Cult Masters: From Bruce Lee To 'Crouching Tiger'*, Wallflower Press, London, 2003
J. Hunter. *Eros In Hell: Sex, Blood and Madness In Japanese Cinema*, Creation Books, London, 1998
J. Inverne. *Musicals*, Faber, London, 2009
L. Irigiaray. *The Irigaray Reader*, ed. M. Whitford, Blackwell, Oxford, 1991
S. Jackson & J. Jones, eds. *Contemporary Feminist Theories*, Edinburgh University Press, Edinburgh, 1998
S. Jaworzyn, ed. *Shock: The Essential Guide To Exploitation Cinema*, Titan Books, London, 1996
S. Jeffords. *Hard Bodies: Hollywood Masculinity In the Reagan Era*, Rutgers University Press, New Brunswick, NJ, 1994
E. Jeffreys & L. Edwards, eds. *Celebrity in China*, Hong Kong University Press, Hong Kong, 2010
K. Kalinak. *Settling the Score: Music and the Classical Hollywood Film*, University of Wisconsin Press, Madison, WI, 1992
B.F. Kawin. *Mindscreen: Bergman, Godard and First-Person Film*, Princeton University Press, Princeton, NJ, 1978
—. *How Movies Work*, Macmillan, New York, NY, 1987
P. Keough, ed. *Flesh and Blood: The National Society of Film Critics on Sex, Violence, and Censorship*, Mercury House, San Francisco, CA, 1995
M. Kinder. *Playing With Power In Movies*, University of California Press, Berkeley, CA, 1991
P. Kolker. *The Altering Eye: Contemporary International Cinema*, Oxford University Press, New York, NY, 1983
—. *A Cinema of Loneliness: Penn, Stone, Kubrick, Scorsese, Spielberg, Altman*, Oxford University Press, New York, NY, 2000
P. Kramer. *The Big Picture: Hollywood Cinema From Star Wars To Titanic*, British Film Institute, London, 2001
—. *The New Hollywood*, Wallflower Press, London, 2005
J. Kristeva. *About Chinese Women*, tr. A. Barrows, Marion Boyars, London, 1977
—. *Desire In Language: A Semiotic Approach To Literature and Art*, ed. L.S. Roudiez, tr. T. Gora *et al*, Blackwell 1982
—. *Powers of Horror: An Essay on Abjection*, tr. L.S. Roudiez, Columbia University Press, New York, NY, 1982
—. *Revolution In Poetic Language*, tr. M. Walker, Columbia University Press, New York, NY, 1984
—. *The Kristeva Reader*, ed. T. Moi, Blackwell, Oxford, 1986
—. *Tales of Love*, tr. L.S. Roudiez, Columbia University Press, New York, NY, 1987
—. *Black Sun: Depression and Melancholy*, tr. L.S. Roudiez, Columbia University Press, New York, NY, 1989
—. *Strangers To Ourselves*, tr. L.S. Roudiez, Harvester Wheatsheaf 1991
J. Kwok Wah Lau. "Imploding Genre, Gender and History: Peking Opera Blues", in J. Geiger, 2005
M. Lanning. *Vietnam At the Movies*, Fawcett Columbine, New York, NY, 1994
R. Lapsley & M. Westlake, eds. *Film Theory: An Introduction*, Manchester University Press, Manchester, 1988
Shing-hou Lau, ed. *A Study of the Hong Kong Martial Arts Film*, Hong Kong International Film Festival, 1980
—. *A Study of the Hong Kong Swordplay Film, 1945-80*, Hong Kong International Film Festival, 1981
Law Kar, ed. *Fifty Years of Elecric Shadows*, Hong Kong International Film Festival, 1997
M. Lee. "*Once Upon a Time In China*", Criterion, 2021
J. Lent. *The Asian Film Industry*, Austin, TX, 1990
T. Leung Siu-hung. "Mastering Action", Hong Kong Cinemagic, March, 2006
E. Levy. *Cinema of Outsiders: The Rise of American Independent Film*, New York University Press, New York, NY, 1999
J. Lewis. *The Road To Romance and Ruin: Teen Films and Youth Culture*, Routledge, London, 1992
—. *Whom God Wishes To Destroy: Francis Coppola and the New Hollywood*, Duke University Press, Durham, NC, 1995
—. ed. *New American Cinema*, Duke University Press, Durham, NC, 1998
—. *Hollywood v. Hard Core: How the Struggle Over Censorship Created the Modern Film Industry*, New York University Press, New York, NY, 2000

J. Leyda. ed. *Film Makers Speak: Voices of Film Experience*, Da Capo, New York, NY, 1977
V. LoBrutto. *Sound-On-Film*, Praeger, New York, NY, 1994
B. Logan. *Hong Kong Action Cinema*, Titan, London, 1995
S. Lu, ed. *Transnational Chinese Cinemas*, University of Hawaii Press, Honolulu, 1997
H. Ludi. *Movie Worlds: Production Design In Film*, Mengers, Stuttgart, 2000
B. McCabe. *The Rough Guide To Comedy Movies*, Rough Guides, London, 2005
R. Maltby. *Harmless Entertainment: Hollywood and the Ideology of Consensus*, Scarecrow Press, Metuchen, NJ, 1983
—. & I. Craven. *Hollywood Cinema: An Introduction*, Blackwell, Oxford, 1995
—. *Hollywood Cinema*, 2nd ed., Blackwell, Oxford, 2003
E. Marks & I. de Courtivron, eds. *New French Feminisms: an anthology*, Harvester Wheatsheaf, Hemel Hempstead, 1981
G. Mast *et al*, eds. *Film Theory and Criticism: Introductory Readings*, Oxford University Press, New York, NY, 1992a
—. & B Kawin. *A Short History of the Movies*, Macmillan, New York, NY, 1992b
C. Marx. *Jet Li*, Martial Arts Masters, Rosen Publishing Group, 2002
T.D. Matthews. *Censored*, Chatto & Windus, London, 1994
F. McConnell. *Storytelling and Mythmaking*, Oxford University Press, New York, NY, 1979
S.Y. McDougal. *Made Into Movies: From Literature To Film*, Holt, Rinehart and Winston, New York, NY, 1985
M. Medved. *Hollywood vs. America*, HarperCollins, London, 1992
R. Meyers. *Martial Arts Movies*, Citadel Press, NJ, 1985
—. *Great Martial Arts Movies*, Citadel Press, NJ, 2001
D. Millar. *Cinema Secrets: Special Effects*, Apple Press, 1990
T. Miller *et al*, eds. *Global Hollywood*, British Film Institute, London, 2001
T. Moi. *Sexual/ Textual Politics: Feminist Literary Theory*, Methuen, London, 1983
J. Monaco. *The New Wave: Truffaut, Godard, Chabrol, Rohmer, Rivette*, Oxford University Press, New York, NY, 1977
—. *American Film Now*, New American Library, London, 1979
—. *How To Read a Film*, Oxford University Press, Oxford, 1981
R. Murray. *Images In the Dark: An Encyclopedia of Gay and Lesbian Film and Video*, Titan Books, London, 1998
S. Neale. *Cinema and Technology*, Macmillan, London, 1985
—. & M. Smith, eds. *Contemporary Hollywood Cinema*, Routledge, London, 1998
—. *Genre and Contemporary Hollywood*, Routledge, London, 2002
J. Nelmes, ed. *An Introduction To Film Studies*, Routledge, London, 1996
D. Neumann, ed. *Film Architecture: From Metropolis To Blade Runner*, Prestel-Verlag, New York, NY, 1996
K. Newman. *Nightmare Movies*, Harmony, New York, NY, 1988
—. *Millennium Movies*, Titan Books, London, 1999
G. Nowell-Smith, ed. *The Oxford History of World Cinema*, Oxford University Press, Oxford, 1996
D. O'Brien. *Spooky Encounters: A Gwailo's Guide To Hong Kong Horror,* Headpress, 2004
T. Ohanian & M. Phillips. *Digital Filmmaking*, 2nd ed., Focal Press, Boston, MA, 2000
J. Orr. *Contemporary Cinema*, Edinburgh University Press, Edinburgh, 1998
B. Palmer *et al*. *The Encyclopedia of Martial Arts Movies*, Scarecrow Press, NJ, 1995
A. Paludan. *Chronicle of the Chinese Emperors*, Thames & Hudson, 1998
L. Pang. *Masculinities and Hong Kong Cinema*, Kent State University Press, 2005
D. Parkinson. *The Rough Guide To Film Musicals*, Penguin, London, 2007
J. Parish. *Jet Li: A Biography*, Thunder's Mouth Press, New York, 2002
F. Patten. *Watching Anime, Reading Manga*, Stone Bridge Press, CA, 2004
D. Peary & G. Peary, eds. *The American Animated Cartoon*, Dutton, New York, NY, 1980
—. *Cult Movies 2*, Vermilion, London, 1984
—. *Cult Movies 3,* Sigwick & Jackson, London, 1989
C. Penley, ed. *Feminism and Film Theory*, Routledge, London, 1988
D. Petrie. *Screening Europe: Image and Identity In Contemporary European Cinema*, British Film Institute, London, 1992
P. Phillips. *Understanding Film Texts*, British Film Institute, London, 2000
M. Pierson. *Special Effects*, Columbia University Press, New York, NY, 2002
L. Pietropaolo & A. Testaferri, eds. *Feminisms In the Cinema*, Indiana University Press, Bloomington, IN, 1995
D. Pollock. *Skywalking: The Life and Films of George Lucas*, Crown, New York, NY, 1983, 1990, 2000
M. Polly. *Bruce Lee*, Simon & Schuster, New York, 2018
S. Prince, ed. *Screening Violence*, Athlone Press, London, 2000
D. Prindle. *Risky Business: The Political Economy of Hollywood*, Westview, Boulder, CO, 1993
N. Proferes. *Film Directing Fundamentals*, Focal Press, Boston, MA, 2001
M. Pye & Lynda Myles. *The Movie Brats: How the Film Generation Took Over Hollywood*, Faber, London, 1979
T. Reeves. *The Worldwide Guide To Movie Locations*, Titan Books, London, 2003

P. Rice & P. Waugh, eds. *Modern Literary Theory: A Reader*, Arnold, London, 1992
D. Richie. *The Films of Akira Kurosawa*, University of California Press, Berkeley, CA, 1965
R. Rickitt. *Special Effects*, Aurum, London, 2006
B. Robb. *Screams and Nightmares*, Titan Books, London, 1998
J. Robertson. *The British Board of Film Censors*, Croom Helm, 1985
D. Robinson. *World Cinema*, Methuen, London, 1981
W.H. Rockett. *Devouring Whirlwind: Terror and Transcendence In the Cinema of Cruelty*, Greenwood Press, New York, NY, 1988
S. Rohdie. *The Passion of Pier Paolo Pasolini*, British Film Institute, London, 1995
J. Romney & A. Wootton, eds. *Celluloid Jukebox: Popular Music and the Movies Since the 50s*, British Film Institute, London, 1995
P. Rosen, ed. *Narrative, Apparatus, Ideology: A Film Theory Reader*, Columbia University Press, New York, NY, 1986
J. Rosenbaum. *Placing Movies*, University of California Press, Berkeley, CA, 1995
R. Rosenblum & R. Karen. *When the Shooting Stops... The Cutting Begins: A Film Editor's Story*, Da Capo Press, New York, NY, 1979
J. Ross. *The Incredibly Strange Film Book: An Alternative History of Cinema*, Simon and Schuster, 1993
The Rough Guide To China, Penguin, 2017
R. Roud. *Jean-Luc Godard*, Thames & Hudson, London, 1970
J. Rovin & K. Tracy. *The Essential Jackie Chan Sourcebook*, Pocket Books, New York, 1997
M. Rubin. *Thrillers*, Cambridge University Press, Cambridge, 1999
K. Russell. *A British Picture: An Autobiography*, Heinemann, London, 1989
V. Russo. *The Celluloid Closet: Homosexuality In the Movies*, Harper & Row, New York, NY, 1981
K. Sandler. *Reading the Rabbit: Explorations In Warner Bros. Animation*, Rutgers University Press, Brunswick, NJ, 1998
A. Sarris. *The American Cinema*, Dutton, New York, NY, 1968
T. Sato. *Currents In Japanese Cinema*, Kodansha, New York, 1982
D. Schaefer & L. Salvato, eds. *Masters of Light*, University of California Press, Berkeley, CA, 1984
T. Schatz. *Hollywood Genres,* Random House, New York, NY, 1981
—. *Old Hollywood/ New Hollywood*, UMI Research Press, Ann Arbor, MI, 1983
—. *The Genius of the System: Hollywood Filmmaking In the Studio Era*, Pantheon, New York, NY 1988
F. Schodt. *Inside the Robot Kingdom: Japan, Mechatronics and the Coming Robotopia*, Kodansha, Tokyo, 1988
—. *Manga! Manga! The World of Japanese Magazines*, Kodansha International, London, 1997
—. *Dreamland Japan: Writings On Modern Manga*, Stone Bridge Press, Berkeley, CA, 2002
P. Schrader. *Transcendental Style In Film: Ozu, Bresson, Dreyer*, Da Capo Press, 1972
A. Schroeder. *Tsui Hark's Zu: Warriors From the Magic Mountain*, Hong Kong University Press, Hong Kong, 2004
R. Schubart. *Super Bitches and Action Babes: The Female Hero In Popular Cinema, 1970-2006*, McFarland, 2007
M. Schumacher. *Francis Ford Coppola*, Bloomsbury, London, 2000
M. Scorsese. *Scorsese On Scorsese*, ed. D. Thompson & I. Christie, Faber, London, 1989, 1995
Screen Reader I: Cinema/ Ideology/ Politics, Society for Education in Film & TV, 1977
Screen Reader II: Cinema and Semiotics, British Film Institute, London, 1982
C. Sharrett, ed. *Crisis Cinema*, Maisonneuve Press, Washington, DC, 1993
—. *Mythologies of Violence In Postmodern Media*, Wayne State University Press, 1999
M. Shiel & T. Fitzmaurice, eds. *Screenng the City*, Verso, London, 2003
D. Shipman. *The Story of Cinema*, Hodder & Stoughton, London, 1984
T. Shone. *Blockbuster: How the Jaws and Jedi Generation Turned Hollywood Into a Boom-Town*, Scribner, London, 2005
E. Showalter, ed. *The New Feminist Criticism*, Virago, London, 1986
E. Siciliano. *Pasolini: A Biography*, Bloomsbury, London, 1987
L. Sider *et al*, eds. *Soundscapes: The School of Sound Lectures 1998-2001*, Wallflower Press, London, 2003
M. Singer. *A History of the American Avant-Garde Cinema*, American Federation of the Arts, New York, NY, 1976
P. Adams Sitney, ed. *The Film Culture Reader*, Praeger, New York, NY, 1970
—. ed. *The Avant-Garde Film: A Reader of Theory and Criticism*, New York University Press, New York, NY, 1978
—. *Visionary Film: The American Avant-Garde, 1943-1978*, 2nd ed., Oxford University Press, New York, NY, 1979
G. Smith. *Epic Films*, McFarland, Jefferson, NC, 1991
J. Smith. *Looking Away: Hollywood and Vietnam*, Scribner's, New York, NY, 1975
T.G. Smith. *Industrial Light and Magic: The Art of Special Effects*, Columbus Books, 1986

E. Smoodin. *Animating Culture: Hollywood Cartoons From the Sound Era*, Roundhouse, 1993
—. ed. *Disney Discourse: Producing the Magic Kingdom*, Routledge, London, 1994
V. Sobchack. *The Limits of Infinity: The American Science Fiction Film*, A.S. Barnes, New York, NY, 1980
—. *Screening Space: The American Science Fiction Film*, Ungar, New York, NY, 1987/ 1993
J. Squire, ed. *The Movie Business Book*, Fireside, New York, NY, 1992
J. Staiger. *Interpreting Films*, Princeton University Press, Princeton, NJ, 1992
—. *Perverse Spectators: The Practices of Film Reception,* New York University Press, New York, NY, 2000
N. Stair. *Michelle Yeoh,* Rosen Publishing Group, 2001
B. Steene. *Ingmar Bergman*, Twayne, Boston, MA, 1968
L. Stern. *The Scorsese Connection*, British Film Institute, London, 1995
D. Sterritt. *The Films of Jean-Luc Godard*, Cambridge University Press, Cambridge, 1999
G. Stewart. *Between Film and Screen: Modernism's Photo Synthesis*, University of Chicago Press, Chicago, IL, 1999
M. Stokes & R. Maltby, eds. *Identifying Hollywood Audiences*, British Film Institute, London, 1999
J. Storey, ed. *Cultural Theory and Popular Culture*, Harvester Wheatsheaf, Hemel Hempstead, 1994
J.M. Straczynski. *The Complete Book of Scriptwriting*, Titan Books, London, 1997
J. Stringer. "Problems With the Treatment of Hong Kong Cinema As Camp", *Asian Cinema*, 8, 2, 1996
—. ed. *Movie Blockbusters*, Routledge, London, 2003
C. Sylvester, ed. *The Penguin Book of Hollywood*, Penguin, London, 1999
K. Tam & W. Dissanayake. *New Chinese Cinema*, Oxford University Press, Hong Kong, 1998
A. Tarkovsky. *Sculpting In Time: Reflections On the Cinema*, tr. K. Hunter-Blair, Faber, London, 1989
C. Tashiro. *Pretty Pictures: Production Design and the History Film,* University of Texas Press, 1998
Y. Tasker. *Spectacular Bodies: Gender, Genre and the Action Cinema*, Routledge, London, 1993
R. Taylor *et al*, eds. *The B.F.I. Companion To Eastern European and Russian Cinema*, British Film Institute, London, 2000
S. Teo. *Hong Kong Cinema*, British Film Institute, London, 1997
—. "Tsui Hark", in C. Yau, 1998
B. Thomas. *Video Hound's Dragon: Asian Action and Cult Flicks*, Visible Ink Press, 2003
K. Thompson & D. Bordwell. *Film History: An Introduction*, McGraw-Hill, New York, NY, 1994/ 2010
—. *Storytelling In the New Hollywood*, Harvard University Press, Cambridge, MA, 1999
D. Thomson. *A Biographical Dictionary of Film,* Deutsch, London, 1995
S. Thrower, ed. *Eyeball: Compendium: Sex and Horror, Art and Exploitation,* F.A.B. Press, Godalming, Surrey, 2003
C. Tohill & P. Tombs. *Immoral Tales: Sex and Horror Cinema In Europe 1956-1984*, Titan Books, London, 1995
J. Trevelyan. *What the Censor Saw*, Michael Joseph, London, 1973
A.D. Vacche. *Cinema and Painting*, Athlone Press, London, 1996
K. Van Gunden. *Fantasy Films*, McFarland, Jefferson, NC 1989
—. *Postmodern Auteurs: Coppola, Lucas, De Palma, Spielberg and Scorsese*, McFarland, Jefferson, NC 1991
M.C. Vaz. *From Star Wars To Indiana Jones*, Chronicle, San Francisco, CA, 1994
—. & P.R. Duignan. *Industrial Light & Magic*, Virgin, London, 1996
G. Vincendeau, ed. *Encyclopedia of European Cinema*, British Film Institute, London, 1995
—. ed. *Film/ Literature/ Heritage: A Sight & Sound Reader*, British Film Institute, London, 2001
P. Virillio. *War and Cinema*, Verso, London, 1992
D. Vivier & T. Podvin. "Through the Lens of Arthur Wong", Hong Kong Cinemagic, Jan 2005
H. Vogel. *Entertainment Industry Economics*, Cambridge University Press, Cambridge, 1995
C. Vogler. *The Writer's Journey: Mythic Structure For Storytellers and Screenwriters*, Pan, London, 1998
J. Wasko. *Movies and Money*, Ablex, NJ, 1982
—. *Hollywood In the Information Age*, Polity Press, Cambridge, 1994
E. Weiss. & J. Belton, eds. *Film Sound: Theory and Practice*, Columbia University Press, New York, NY, 1989
T. Weisser. *Asian Cult Cinema*, Boulevard Books, New York, NY, 1997
O. Welles. *This is Orson Welles*, HarperCollins, London, 1992
P. Wells. *Understanding Animation*, Routledge, London, 1998
D. West. *Chasing Dragons: An Introduction To the Martial Arts Film*, I.B. Tauris, London, 2006
L. Williams, ed. *Viewing Positions: Ways of Seeing Film*, Rutgers University Press, New

Brunswick, NJ, 1995
T. Williams. "To Live and Die In Hong Kong", *Cineaction*, 36, 1995
—. "Kwan Tak-hing and the New Generation", *Asian Cinema*, 10, 1, 1998
—. "Space, Place and Spectacle: the Crisis Cinema of John Woo", in P. Fu, 2002
R. Witterstaetter. *Dying For Action: The Life and Times of Jackie Chan*, Warner Books, New York, 1997
M. Wolf. *The Entertainment Economy*, Penguin, London, 1999
P. Wollen: *Signs and Meaning In the Cinema*, Secker & Warburg, London, 1972
J. Woo. Interview, in J. Arroyo, 2000
—. *Interviews; Conversations With Filmmakers Series*, ed. R. Elder, University Press of Mississippi, 2005
M. Wood. *Cine East: Hong Kong Cinema Through the Looking Glass*, F.A.B. Press, 1998
R. Wood. *Hollywood From Vietnam To Reagan... and Beyond*, Columbia University Press, New York, NY, 2003
T. Woods. *Beginning Postmodernism*, Manchester University Press, Manchester, 1999
J. Wyatt. *High Concept: Movies and Marketing In Hollywood*, University of Texas Press, Austin, TX, 1994
J. Yang et al. *Eastern Standard Time: A Guide To Asian Influence On American Culture*, Houghton Mifflin, Boston, MA, 1997
—. *Once Upon a Time In China*, Atria Books, New York, NY, 2003
E.C.M. Yau, ed. *At Full Speed: Hong Kong Cinema In a Borderless World*, University of Minnesota Press, Minneapolis, MN, 1998
Z. Yimou. *Zhang Yimou: Interviews, Conversations With Filmmakers Series*, ed. F. Gateward, University Press of Mississippi, 2001
Judith T. Zeitlin. *Historian of the Strange: Pu Songling and the Chinese Classical Tale*, Stanford University Press, Stanford, CA, 1993
Y. Zhang & X. Zhiwei, eds. *Encyclopedia of Chinese Film*, Routledge, 1998
J. Zipes. *The Enchanted Screen: The Unknown History of Fairy-tale Films*, Routledge, New York, NY, 2011
S. Zizek. *Enjoy Your Symptom Jacques Lacan In Hollywood and Out*, Routledge, New York, NY, 1992
—. *The Fright of Real Tears: The Uses and Misuses of Lacan In Film Theory*, British Film Institute, London, 1999

JEREMY ROBINSON has published poetry, fiction, and studies of J.R.R. Tolkien, Samuel Beckett, Thomas Hardy, André Gide and D.H. Lawrence. Robinson has edited poetry books by Novalis, Ursula Le Guin, Friedrich Hölderlin, Francesco Petrarch, Dante Alighieri, Arseny Tarkovsky, and Rainer Maria Rilke.

Books on film and animation include: *The Akira Book* • *The Art of Katsuhiro Otomo* • *The Art of Masamune Shirow* • *The Ghost In the Shell Book* • *Fullmetal Alchemist* • *Cowboy Bebop: The Anime and Movie* • *The Cinema of Hayao Miyazaki* • *Hayao Miyazaki: Pocket Guide* • *Princess Mononoke: Pocket Movie Guide* • *Spirited Away: Pocket Movie Guide* • *Blade Runner and the Cinema of Philip K. Dick* • *Blade Runner: Pocket Movie Guide* • *The Cinema of Donald Cammell* • *Performance: Donald Cammell: Nic Roeg: Pocket Movie Guide* • *Pasolini: Il Cinema di Poesia/ The Cinema of Poetry* • *Salo: Pocket Movie Guide* • *The Trilogy of Life Movies: Pocket Movie Guide* • *The Gospel According To Matthew: Pocket Movie Guide* • *The Ecstatic Cinema of Tony Ching Siu-tung* • *Tsui Hark: The Dragon Master of Chinese Cinema* • *The Swordsman: Pocket Movie Guide* • *A Chinese Ghost Story: Pocket Movie Guide* • *Ken Russell: England's Great Visionary Film Director and Music Lover* • *Tommy: Ken Russell: The Who: Pocket Movie Guide* • *Women In Love: Ken Russell: D.H. Lawrence: Pocket Movie Guide* • *The Devils: Ken Russell: Pocket Movie Guide* • *Walerian Borowczyk: Cinema of Erotic Dreams* • *The Beast: Pocket Movie Guide* • *The Lord of the Rings Movies* • *The Fellowship of the Ring: Pocket Movie Guide* • *The Two Towers: Pocket Movie Guide* • *The Return of the King: Pocket Movie Guide* • *Jean-Luc Godard: The Passion of Cinema* • *The Sacred Cinema of Andrei Tarkovsky* • *Andrei Tarkovsky: Pocket Guide*.

'It's amazing for me to see my work treated with such passion and respect. There is nothing resembling it in the U.S. in relation to my work.'
(Andrea Dworkin)

'This model monograph – it is an exemplary job, and I'm very proud that he has accorded me a couple of mentions… The subject matter of his book is beautifully organised and dead on beam.'
(Lawrence Durrell, on *The Light Eternal: A Study of J.M.W. Turner*)

'Jeremy Robinson's poetry is certainly jammed with ideas, and I find it very interesting for that reason. It's certainly a strong imprint of his personality.'
(Colin Wilson)

'*Sex-Magic-Poetry-Cornwall* is a very rich essay… It is a very good piece… vastly stimulating and insightful.'
(Peter Redgrove)

CRESCENT MOON PUBLISHING

web: www.crmoon.com e-mail: cresmopub@yahoo.co.uk

ARTS, PAINTING, SCULPTURE

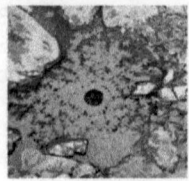

The Art of Andy Goldsworthy
Andy Goldsworthy: Touching Nature
Andy Goldsworthy in Close-Up
Andy Goldsworthy: Pocket Guide
Andy Goldsworthy In America
Land Art: A Complete Guide
The Art of Richard Long
Richard Long: Pocket Guide
Land Art In the UK
Land Art in Close-Up
Land Art In the U.S.A.
Land Art: Pocket Guide
Installation Art in Close-Up
Minimal Art and Artists In the 1960s and After
Colourfield Painting
Land Art DVD, TV documentary
Andy Goldsworthy DVD, TV documentary

The Erotic Object: Sexuality in Sculpture From Prehistory to the Present Day
Sex in Art: Pornography and Pleasure in Painting and Sculpture
Postwar Art
Sacred Gardens: The Garden in Myth, Religion and Art
Glorification: Religious Abstraction in Renaissance and 20th Century Art
Early Netherlandish Painting
Leonardo da Vinci
Piero della Francesca
Giovanni Bellini
Fra Angelico: Art and Religion in the Renaissance
Mark Rothko: The Art of Transcendence
Frank Stella: American Abstract Artist
Jasper Johns
Brice Marden

Alison Wilding: The Embrace of Sculpture
Vincent van Gogh: Visionary Landscapes
Eric Gill: Nuptials of God
Constantin Brancusi: Sculpting the Essence of Things
Max Beckmann
Caravaggio
Gustave Moreau

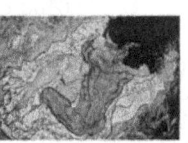

Egon Schiele: Sex and Death In Purple Stockings
Delizioso Fotografico Fervore: Works In Process 1
Sacro Cuore: Works In Process 2
The Light Eternal: J.M.W. Turner
The Madonna Glorified: Karen Arthurs

MEDIA, CINEMA, FEMINISM and CULTURAL STUDIES

J.R.R. Tolkien: The Books, The Films, The Whole Cultural Phenomenon
J.R.R. Tolkien: Pocket Guide
The *Lord of the Rings* Movies: Pocket Guide
The Cinema of Hayao Miyazaki
Hayao Miyazaki: *Princess Mononoke*: Pocket Movie Guide
Hayao Miyazaki: *Spirited Away*: Pocket Movie Guide
Tim Burton : Hallowe'en For Hollywood
Ken Russell
Ken Russell: *Tommy*: Pocket Movie Guide
The Ghost Dance: The Origins of Religion
The Peyote Cult
Cixous, Irigaray, Kristeva: The *Jouissance* of French Feminism
Julia Kristeva: Art, Love, Melancholy, Philosophy, Semiotics and Psychoanalysis
Luce Irigaray: Lips, Kissing, and the Politics of Sexual Difference
Hélene Cixous I Love You: The *Jouissance* of Writing
Andrea Dworkin
'Cosmo Woman': The World of Women's Magazines
Women in Pop Music
HomeGround: The Kate Bush Anthology
Discovering the Goddess (Geoffrey Ashe)
The Poetry of Cinema
The Sacred Cinema of Andrei Tarkovsky
Andrei Tarkovsky: Pocket Guide
Andrei Tarkovsky: *Mirror*: Pocket Movie Guide
Andrei Tarkovsky: *The Sacrifice*: Pocket Movie Guide
Walerian Borowczyk: Cinema of Erotic Dreams
Jean-Luc Godard: The Passion of Cinema
Jean-Luc Godard: *Hail Mary*: Pocket Movie Guide
Jean-Luc Godard: *Contempt*: Pocket Movie Guide
Jean-Luc Godard: *Pierrot le Fou*: Pocket Movie Guide
John Hughes and Eighties Cinema
Ferris Bueller's Day Off: Pocket Movie Guide
Jean-Luc Godard: Pocket Guide
The Cinema of Richard Linklater
Liv Tyler: Star In Ascendance
Blade Runner and the Films of Philip K. Dick
Paul Bowles and Bernardo Bertolucci
Media Hell: Radio, TV and the Press
An Open Letter to the BBC
Detonation Britain: Nuclear War in the UK
Feminism and Shakespeare
Wild Zones: Pornography, Art and Feminism
Sex in Art: Pornography and Pleasure in Painting and Sculpture
Sexing Hardy: Thomas Hardy and Feminism

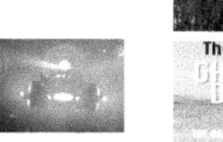

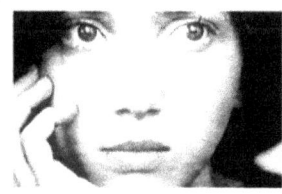

The Light Eternal is a model monograph, an exemplary job. The subject matter of the book is beautifully organised and dead on beam. (Lawrence Durrell)

It is amazing for me to see my work treated with such passion and respect. (Andrea Dworkin)

CRESCENT MOON PUBLISHING
P.O. Box 1312, Maidstone, Kent, ME14 5XU, Great Britain. www.crmoon.com

cresmopub@yahoo.co.uk   www.crescentmoon.org.uk

www.ingramcontent.com/pod-product-compliance
Lightning Source LLC
Chambersburg PA
CBHW060535100426
42743CB00009B/1534